José-Maria de Heredia

By ALVIN HARMS

University of Calgary

TWAYNE PUBLISHERS

A DIVISION OF G. K. HALL & CO., BOSTON

Library of Congress Cataloging in Publication Data

Harms, Alvin.
  José-Maria de Heredia.

  (Twayne's world authors series; TWAS 347: France)
  Bibliography: p. 155.
  Includes index.
  1. Heredia, José María de, 1842-1905.
PQ2275.H3Z64   843'.8   74-22312
ISBN 0-8057-2421-4

Contents

About the Author

Alvin Harms received his B.A. Honors from the University of Saskatchewan and his Ph.D. from the University of Colorado. He pioneered in setting up French studies at the young University of Calgary and was the first head of its Department of Romance Studies, where he is now Professor of French. Professor Harms's special interests lie in Romanticism, lyric poetry generally and poetic theory. His publications include articles on Lamartine and Leconte de Lisle.

Preface

It has never seemed to me to be possible to form a true picture of a writer on the basis of a few anthology pieces. Yet it is likely that many amateurs of French literature have had no other contact with Heredia. He is not widely read, not much studied and not very well known these days. I offer this book in the hope that it will give readers at least a basic notion of this poet and his work, in so far as this is possible in a small volume. There are few existing books on Heredia. Perhaps there is really only one complete study of him, and that is Miodrag Ibrovac's book entitled *José-Maria de Heredia. Sa Vie, son oeuvre*. It is exhaustive, rich and meticulously documented, so that one would think nothing more could be added. However, it is not recent, dating from 1923, and since it is written in French it is not accessible to all readers on this continent. To my knowledge no book in English has yet appeared on Heredia.

In attempting to present my personal judgment of Heredia's work and the possible reactions of our time to it, I have tried to resist the temptation to attribute to him a greater importance than he deserves. At the same time I feel that the lyricism of his poetry has too often been underestimated. I have been sustained in my work by my admiration of much that is good in his writings: consistently elevated utterance, peerless workmanship, high ideals, and above all its serene and sensitive humanity. Although Heredia is known to many solely as the author of a book of sonnets, I have tried to present an idea of his prose as well.

It is my feeling that Heredia's life is not very well known on this continent. Most of the biographical material is in the first three chapters and attempts to situate him within the literary currents of his time. If Chapter 4 is somewhat long, it is because I am assuming that some readers will not have read *Les Trophées* in their entirety. I have therefore tried to provide a fairly full notion of their content, but I hope my remarks are interpretive as well. Chapter 5 develops my view that *Les Trophées* have an underlying elegiac character. My treatment of his poetic art in Chapter 6 in no way aspires to be definitive or exhaustive. I have addressed myself in large part to the questions of artistic structure and verbal patterns. Questions of a statistical nature, as for example percentage of rich rhymes, are largely untouched here and have been dealt with by Ibrovac and also in Heinrich Fromm's dissertation for the University of Greifswald, 1913, entitled *"Les Trophées" von José-Maria de Heredia. Untersuchungen über den Aufbau, Reim und Stil.*

The translations of quotations I have used are my own. On the whole they tend to be literal and where they translate Heredia's verse they do not pretend to reflect its poetic qualities. Unless otherwise stated all quotations from the *Trophées* are taken from José-Maria de Heredia, *Les Trophées*, Paris: Lemerre, n.d. [1893].

Finally I acknowledge with gratitude the help given to me for the preparation of this study by the Canada Council through a research grant.

ALVIN HARMS

University of Calgary

Chronology

July 21, and at the unveiling of Du Bellay's statue, September 2.

1895 Delivered his reception address in the French Academy, May 30. Became literary director of *Le Journal*.

1900 Represented the French Academy at the unveiling of Maupassant's monument at Rouen.

1901 Became a correspondent for *El Pais*. Was appointed administrator of the Bibliothèque de l'Arsenal.

1902 Presided at the commemoration of Victor Hugo's centenary.

1905 Died October 2 at Condé-sur-Vesgres. Funeral ceremony held, October 6. Interred at Rouen in the cemetery of Notre-Dame-de-Bon-Secours, October 7.

CHAPTER 1

The Beginnings

J OSE-MARIA de Heredia was born on November 22, 1842, in a valley of the Sierra Maestra not far from Santiago, on the southern coast of Cuba, looking out over the ocean toward Jamaica. His birthplace was the coffee plantation of La Fortuna, one of two plantations owned by the Heredia family on the island (the other one was called Le Potosi). Like the family of the Creole poet Leconte de Lisle, who was to have such a large influence on Heredia later, the Heredias were planters, and successful ones at that. The name La Fortuna could almost be considered symbolical, like a happy star presiding over the destiny of the poet. Not only did the family plantations assure him a certain financial independence later, but his life as a whole was relatively free of major tragedies. Others might well have envied him his general good fortune in his literary activities, his social relationships and the many assets with which nature had endowed him at birth.

I *Origins*

José-Maria de Heredia is no ordinary name. His double given name is the Spanish form of the names of Christ's parents. His whole name has such a proud ring and solid symmetry that we are hardly astonished to learn that it is associated with a long and distinguished history. José-Maria's ancestors can be traced to the Spanish *conquistadores* on his father's side and to the French Vikings on his mother's side. The Heredias originated in southern Spain and the poet's paternal ancestors settled in North America in the sixteenth century. While there appear to be some uncertainties in the more remote chapters of the family history, the real founder of the Heredia line may have been Jean-Ferdinand de Heredia, Grand Master of the Order of Rhodes, born in the early part of the fourteenth century. His career, however, was linked with France: he

fought at the battle of Crécy, became governor of Avignon, had for-
tifications built, and was the friend of Pope Innocent VI. Another
Heredia, Don Pedro, took part in an expedition to the Indies with
Christopher Columbus' brother Bartholomew. He was given the
governorship of a province in 1532, founded Carthagena, which he
named after his native village in Aragon, and later lost his life in a
shipwreck off the coast of Florida. His son Don Manuel inherited
from him the province of Bani on the island of Santo Domingo. This
property was still in the Heredia family in the eighteenth century, at
which time it was under the control of three brothers, descendants of
Don Manuel: Don José-Francisco, Don Domingo and Don Ignacio.[1]

During the French Revolution native insurrections, especially the
revolt of Toussaint-Louverture, drove the whites out of Santo
Domingo. Ruined by these uprisings the Heredias took refuge in
Cuba along with other families, both Spanish and French, which
were similarly affected. In this way Spanish and French colonists
came to settle side by side and eventually to intermingle. Of the
three Heredia brothers, only the two older ones deserve our attention here. Each of them had a son named José-Maria and both of
these sons later became poets. Don José-Francisco's son, born in
1803, gained some renown as a Spanish language poet and died in
1839, an exile in Mexico. The younger José-Maria, who is the subject
of this study, was the son of the second brother, Don Domingo, an
energetic, proud and enterprising man who spared no effort to
restore the family fortune. Notwithstanding his aristocratic
background, he went so far as to work on La Fortuna and Le Potosi
with his own hands. His family was fairly large: by his first wife he
had one daughter and three sons, and after remarrying in 1830
fathered three more daughters and one son. The last son was the
youngest child, named José-Maria.

On his father's side José-Maria's illustrious ancestry evokes images
of men of action, dauntless and intrepid adventurers, explorers and
colonizers, men of robust temperament fashioned in the mold of
"stout Cortez." His mother's family, though it could not equal his
father's in flamboyance and excitement, was nonetheless not lacking
in distinction.[2] His mother, Louise Girard by her maiden name, was
French of Norman extraction. Her great grandfather Girard
d'Ouville, a nobleman, had been president of the *Parlement* of Normandy under Louis XV. His son, thanks to the influence of Madame
de Pompadour, who was his godmother, obtained an important post

on the island of Santo Domingo. Thus the Girard family, like the Heredias, was among the early European colonists of the New World. And like the Heredias, the Girards also took refuge in Cuba and established plantations there.

II *Childhood*

José-Maria de Heredia's life began in happy circumstances. His childhood was not marked by the loneliness, unwholesome sensitivity, morbid daydreaming, poverty, or unhappy family relationships that darkened the early years of many well-known poets. As the youngest child he seems to have enjoyed all the advantages of his position without experiencing many of its drawbacks. He was the center of affection in the family. Not only did he enjoy the attention of his four older sisters and of his parents, but he had numerous aunts and cousins, memories of whom were later evoked by his daughter Gérard d'Houville in her poem "Stances aux dames créoles." Even visitors to the house found him charming and handsome. Yet in spite of all the attention lavished on him he remained relatively unspoiled, an obedient and likable child who had the gift of making friends, a gift he maintained throughout his life.

His parents treated him gently. He knew no severe restraints and his early years were not too rigidly regulated. It is likely that his parents cared deeply for him and tried to rear him in a Christian manner. His father was somewhat taciturn and lacked the warmth of José-Maria's mother. Every night when he said good-night to his father he would find Don Domingo reading his breviary. He would kiss his father's extended hand and then receive his benediction before going to bed.[3]

His island home must have seemed like a tropical paradise to José-Maria; he loved its exotic flora, and he was free to roam and to explore the sinuous paths through the wooded mountain slope, typical then of the terrain of the province of Santiago, and to experience intimately its beauty. From La Fortuna the family later moved to Le Potosi, noted for its terraced gardens and beautiful flowers, both tropical and European.[4] Heredia may have been reliving memories of this island beauty when in later years he used to take walks through the Luxembourg gardens in Paris. The charm of his island remained with him all his life. The Spanish title *El Pais* of a journal with which he collaborated later reminded him once again of his home and elicited from him this beautiful and moving testimonial:

Il me ramène à l'île éclatante et lointaine où je suis né. Je revois les riches montagnes de la *Sierre Madre* qui dominent la baie de Santiago de Cuba, la maison paternelle, entourée d'orangers, de citronniers et de lauriers-roses, le jardin plein de colibris, d'oiseaux mouches et de fleurs; je crois respirer encore l'odeur de jasmin des caféiers en fleurs, je suis le cours du Bacanao qui roule là-bas, dans un lit de marbre, ses eaux claires à l'ombre des cocotiers, des manguiers et des hauts bambous frémissants à la moindre brise. . . .[5]

It takes me back to the bright and distant island where I was born. I see again the rich Sierra Madre mountains which dominate Santiago Bay, Cuba, the family home, surrounded by orange trees, by lemon trees and laurel roses, the garden full of humming birds, colibris and flowers. It seems as if I smell again the fragrance of jasmine, of coffee plants in bloom, I follow the course of the Bacanao which flows in the distance in its bed of marble, with its clear waters in the shadow of the cocoa trees, the mango trees and the tall bamboo shivering in the slightest breeze. . . .

But this fairy-tale boyhood in which he was a kind of Prince Charming was soon to end. His parents recognized that José-Maria was a child of precocious intelligence and sensitivity. Even as a small boy he was preoccupied with fundamental questions of love and death. He was talented, having already learned to dance, play the guitar and ride. His parents, themselves people of culture, wanted to give him the best education possible. They realized that to keep the boy on the island would be tantamount to condemning him to a kind of intellectual stagnation, and so they decided to send him to France under the guardianship of a certain Nicolas Fauvelle, a refined and cultivated man, formerly also a planter in Cuba as well as a business associate and close friend of Domingo de Heredia. He had since returned to France to his native town of Senlis, but the Heredias remembered that on learning of José-Maria's birth Fauvelle had offered his services toward the boy's education. They now decided to take advantage of the offer.

An unexpected event delayed this step. Don Domingo, who had been ailing, decided to go to France for his health, but before reaching his destination he died at sea on April 15, 1849. For a time it seemed as if this unexpected tragedy would nullify the plans to provide José-Maria with an education in France. The death of her husband was a blow from which Madame Heredia never quite recovered. However, she was a woman of courage and quality. She found consolation in her children and she gradually took over her husband's business affairs, proving in time to be a capable manager of the plantation. A cultivated, affectionate and sensitive woman, she was unwilling to abandon her dream of a French education for her son. On the other hand, the latter's departure would have meant separation from the only surviving male member of her family. In all probability she envisaged his role in the days after her husband's death as the eventual administrator of the plantation.

It was another unexpected event that helped her come to a decision. Fauvelle, who had just lost his wife, came to Cuba for a visit, during the course of which he persuaded Madame Heredia to let him take her son back to France with him. Accordingly in October, 1851, José-Maria, not quite nine years of age, left his island home with Fauvelle, a man who now became a substitute for his father and whom he accepted very quickly in that role.

III *Education*

The impressive erudition of the mature José-Maria de Heredia was in part the product of some important early influences. His keen mind found fertile ground in the home atmosphere created by his parents. Fauvelle fortunately was able to continue providing suitable intellectual stimuli. An intelligent man and somewhat of a philosopher interested in all facets of the life of the mind, he had a very fine personal library. It was under his supervision that José-Maria's formal education in France began with the Fathers of the Beauvais Diocese in the Catholic College Saint-Vincent at Senlis situated in Oise not many miles north of Paris.

This school taught humanities in preparation for the baccalaureate. This was exactly the type of basic education Heredia's father had imagined for his son. Madame Heredia was eager that this ambition be realized before her son made a choice of profession. The school had a good reputation. It was natural that José-Maria was somewhat lonely at first but his first impressions of fear and abandonment were soon dispelled. He adapted rapidly and his progress was all that could have been wished. The calm and harmonious landscape around the school was conducive to his meditations. The fathers and sisters teaching him treated him well and he enjoyed the company of his comrades. He appears to have been a well-balanced, normal boy, as eager to participate in sports (especially handball, football and a version of baseball) as to pursue intellectual interests. He was an excellent student and worked hard. His favorite subjects were dead languages, history, and French, interests directly related to and reflected in his later poetry. Generally he was near the top in his class and his successes were rewarded by a number of prizes.

The eight years he spent at Senlis left him many pleasant

memories. Years later when he was already beginning to be recognized in literary circles he was invited to speak at a banquet of alumni of Saint-Vincent. On that occasion he spoke with affection of the "big happy family" of his school days there, paid tribute to his teachers, and reminisced about the mischievous pranks characteristic of school boys everywhere and which he still remembered so well. He stressed the quality of the education which the school had given. At the entrance to the school there is a plaque in honor of Heredia and on it are inscribed the following words, which he had spoken on the occasion of that reunion:

> Nous avons appris à aimer
> Tout ce qui est bon, tout ce qui est beau,
> La Religion, la Nature, l'Art, la Patrie
> Et de plus d'un étranger
> Saint-Vincent a fait un Français.

Here we learned to love all that is good, all that is beautiful, Religion, Nature, Art, Fatherland, and of more than one foreigner Saint-Vincent has made a Frenchman.

Perhaps no other comment could have summed up so well his own ideals.

His stay at Senlis came to an end in May 1859. He had obtained his baccalaureate on November 9, 1858, but he did not want to go away. It was like leaving home. Besides his happy school experiences he had had the pleasure of a number of summer trips to the Pyrenees area, visiting aunts and cousins.[6] However, no useful purpose could be served by prolonging his stay. His future was uncertain. During these eight years his mother had been in constant correspondence with Fauvelle and with her son, and had followed the latter's progress with keen interest, concern and pleasure. She had been considering various possibilities for him. Perhaps he ought to continue his education at the Ecole Polytechnique. On the other hand, why not send him to a business firm in Bordeaux or Spain to learn Spanish, bookkeeping and business administration so he could return to Cuba and take charge of the plantation? And yet she was not altogether convinced that he should make the management of the plantation his career. After all, that was not, in her opinion, a really noble profession. Such were the thoughts she entertained during José-Maria's absence.

She had planned to go to France for her son's graduation, expecting then to return to Cuba with him. Unfortunately ill health kept her in Cuba, and so on June 10, 1859, José-Maria arrived in Le Potosi by himself. By this time his mother had decided that perhaps he could temporarily participate in the administration of the plantation while planning a career in law, for which he could undertake studies in Havana.

José-Maria dutifully consented to follow this plan. Because she considered her son to be at an impressionable age, Madame Heredia had some misgivings about sending him away to Havana where he would be without a counsellor. However, in addition to being an obedient son, he seems to have been both reasonable and practical. Moreover, he had a sense of honor. His father at one time had wanted to study law, a profession which he considered honorable.[7] Still, José-Maria was not completely enthusiastic about it all. He found plantation life repugnant, yet obtained pleasure from his visits with relatives and from his attempts to perfect his Spanish.

In September 1859 he went to Havana. He was soon bored with Cuban society. Apparently the Faculty of Law refused to admit him, not recognizing his baccalaureate diploma as official. Instead of law studies he found himself taking another step toward what was eventually to be his real career, by undertaking studies in philosophy and literature. His rapid progress in Spanish was amazing. Moreover, he was a voracious reader, discussed literature tirelessly and gained considerable familiarity with Spanish literature.

Havana quickly outlived its usefulness to him. In the long run it could not offer him the way of life for which he yearned. For some time he and his mother had been planning to return to France. Heredia was impatient to leave. On April 15, 1861, they finally departed, taking with them a small orange tree in a bit of the "cherished earth" from the plantation. Heredia was destined never to see Cuba again.

After a fifty day crossing they disembarked at Bordeaux. For Heredia it was like a homecoming. His mother, on the other hand, was homesick at first. She relied more and more on her son in the management of practical affairs and he, for his part, showed himself competent. After several weeks of visiting in the Pyrenees, mother and son reached Paris and before the end of July José-Maria had made all the arrangements for furniture and an apartment for them.

The next chapter in Heredia's formal education began on November 4, 1861, with his enrolment to study law. He took part in student activities and became briefly interested in politics, all the while working conscientiously on his law program. But it was becoming increasingly clear that his future lay neither in politics nor in law. In fact, he was beginning to dislike law intensely.

In November, 1862, Heredia finally discovered a solution to his problem. He entered the Ecole Nationale des Chartes. This institution trained librarians and archivists. It taught such skills and subject matter as paleography, the deciphering of manuscripts and inscriptions, old languages including Vulgar Latin, medieval history, and heraldry. Clearly it looked to the past and its value was to supply the tools for research into the past, especially medieval times. During these years Heredia allowed himself to be sidetracked at times by other activities, such as visits to Italy and Spain and travels in Brittany, so that he was never able to concentrate on the academic exercise of completing the required thesis. It appears that at least on one occasion he asked for an extension of time for his thesis and for permission to change his subject. However, the project was never completed. Although he was always among the best students, Heredia did not obtain his diploma.[8]

As the family fortune was adequate, he did not feel compelled to seek employment. And perhaps he was already beginning vaguely to notice the first beckoning of the Muses. What he obtained from the school was far more valuable than a diploma. The institution aroused and reinforced in him a love and an understanding of the past, intensified his curiosity and developed in him a taste for precision; in short, it made him a trained historian. While it prepared most of its graduates for more or less practical careers, it affected Heredia's career in a more indirect way. It did not make him a poet, but it played a role in leading him toward the past as a source of inspiration.

Meanwhile, during the three or four years he was at the Ecole Nationale des Chartes he had not entirely abandoned his law studies. For the sake of the family especially he dutifully and doggedly continued. Although he failed his examinations at his first try in 1863, he obtained his baccalaureate in law the following year and even took his licentiate examinations in 1866. His formal education was now ended.

IV *Beginnings of a Poetic Vocation*

At this point Heredia was in his middle twenties. He was ready for his life work. Endowed with an optimistic outlook, energetic, handsome, aristocratic, and now solidly prepared academically, he must have been impatient to plunge into the world of action. And action for him meant first and foremost intellectual activity, specifically of a creative order.

But what made Heredia become a poet rather than a lawyer or a businessman? A partial answer to this question is that plantation life simply was not to his liking and that law, notwithstanding its prestige in the Heredia family, did not interest him. On the other hand, a number of influences in his early life in all likelihood encouraged him in the direction of poetry. The numerous stimuli provided by the rich natural life of Cuba may well have intensified his sensitivity toward color, form and natural beauty. Moreover his taste for refined and beautiful things originated in his boyhood home with the influence of his parents.

In fact it was Madame Heredia who introduced him to French verse, specifically that of Lamartine. In his address to the French Academy many years later on the occasion of his formal reception, Heredia was to recall vividly the impact which that poet had made on him:

Lamartine! Son nom doucement sonore est le premier nom de poète qui ait caressé mon oreille. Ses vers sont les premiers que ma mémoire ait retenus lorsque, tout petit enfant, je m'agenouillais dans le grand lit maternel et que, joignant les mains, je récitais mot par mot, suivant une voix bien chère qui s'est tue depuis bien longtemps, la prière matinale:
> "O Père qu'adore mon père!
> Toi qu'on ne nomme qu'à genoux!
> Toi dont le nom terrible et doux
> Fait courber le front de ma mère!"[9]

Lamartine! His gently sonorous name is the first poet's name to caress my ears. His verse is the first my mind can remember when, as a very small child, I kneeled on my mother's large bed and, folding my hands, I repeated word for word after a voice very dear to me but long ago silent, the morning prayer: "O Father whom my father adores! Thou whom we name only on bended knee! Thou whose name both terrible and gentle makes my mother bow her head!"

So great was the impression Lamartine made on him that he appears all his life to have preserved a great admiration for him. One wonders whether it is not more than mere coincidence that Heredia's *Trophées* contain 118 sonnets, exactly the same number as the number of pages in the first edition of Lamartine's *Méditations poétiques*.[10]

Heredia's eight years at Senlis intensified his contact with the humanities and allowed him to discover other poets. Apparently he began to dabble in poetry during this time. In a letter of October 29, 1860, addressed to Fauvelle, he recalls that while at the Collège Saint-Vincent he had "teased the Muses".[11] It is not clear what he wrote there but indications are that he attempted some fragments of epic poetry. In any event his work was not yet very serious.

Only after his graduation from Saint-Vincent did his poetic vocation begin to define itself more sharply. It was another nineteenth-century French poet who gave considerable impetus to Heredia's poetic development. On the very day of his graduation, as he was walking past a bookstore, his eyes fell upon a collection of verse whose cover was arrestingly illustrated. He bought the book and began to look through it while continuing to walk. That volume happened to be a collection of Leconte de Lisle's verse. On the voyage back to Cuba a few months later Heredia read these poems over and over and continued to reread them on the plantation and in Havana. Leconte de Lisle was a revelation for him. He had discovered the poet who was to become his master. Although he had not yet met the man, his contact with the latter's poetry was the first step toward one of the very close associations recorded by literary history between two writers.

Besides Leconte de Lisle's poetry, Heredia now read Chateaubriand, Ronsard, and Hugo, especially the latter's *Légende des siècles*. It would of course be too simplistic to think that the character of Heredia's poetry was determined solely by these four writers. On the other hand, each of these four almost certainly left his mark in Heredia's apprenticeship. The *Légende des siècles* impressed him greatly. He had written a few fragments of epic poetry, but so overawed was he by Hugo's *Légende* that he abandoned the longer epic and chose the sonnet, a form which Hugo had not used for his epic poetry.[12]

V Early Poems

The first of Heredia's poems that have been preserved dates from the time he spent in Cuba after his graduation from the Collège Saint-Vincent. It was written in 1859 apparently to mark the tenth anniversary of his father's death. Entitled "A mon père dont les cheveux avaient blanchi avant l'âge" (To my father whose hair had grown white prematurely), it is clearly not the work of a mature poet. Its point of departure is the Christian concept that the pious can die in peace because the tomb is the beginning of another life, while for the evil the prospect of death is a dreaded one. It goes without saying that Heredia places his father into the first category, and he expresses the hope that his faith will be equally strong. The poem is really a kind of ode, which appears somewhat inflated perhaps because it is written in the elevated tone conventionally reserved for great public and heroic figures. It ends with a somewhat extravagant image suggesting that his father's white hair symbolizes nobility just as the snow on the summit of a volcanic mountain is pure because it is closer to heaven. Technically, the poem is uneven; its stanzaic patterns are inconsistent and its rhymes mixed.

The second poem of which we have a record is entitled "A la fontaine de la India," and its first version is dated Havana, March 5, 1860. This is Heredia's first sonnet, the form in which he was later to distinguish himself and which he was to use almost exclusively. Whereas "A mon père dont les cheveux avaient blanchi avant l âge" contains certain accents of the late eighteenth and early nineteenth-century ode, this sonnet has in it echoes of the Romantic poets, in particular Lamartine and Hugo. The opening lines, for example, recall Lamartine's "L'Isolement." However, the central feeling here is not love of one human being for another, but love for Cuba, and the theme of solitude is not developed. The poem expresses the pleasure of meditating alone beside the fountain. The latter appears to become animate and leads the poet to reflect on his love for the beauty of the island as a whole. A major weakness of this poem, in my opinion, is its lack of unity of tone and conception. On the one hand it evokes an evening moonlit scene and personal reactions to that scene; on the other hand the fountain is apostrophized as a lover of the sun and its form suggests that of a chiseled marble statue. It is clear that Heredia's esthetics had not yet been defined. The subjective approach, the vague, the nocturnal, and the love of reverie were all elements to be found in the Romantic poets he had been reading. But the emergence of an interest in sculptured outlines and sunlit landscapes announced a direction he and many of his contemporaries were to follow.

It is also worth noting that Heredia already shows considerable skill in handling the sonnet. It is on the whole tightly constructed. The fountain he contemplates in the octave is transformed in the sestet to symbolize the whole island in its exotic beauty. The last verse, "Les murmures d 'amour de tes nuits lumineuses" (The murmurs of love of your luminous nights), leaves the reader with a memorable impression of that beauty, both sensual and affective.

The effort to make the last verse especially striking is perhaps one of the characteristics of the sonnet form in particular, but for Heredia it was a technique which he perfected to such a degree that it has almost become a trademark of his verse.

In the summer of 1860 Heredia was working on a longer poem, "Les Bois américains," of which he sent a fifty-six verse fragment to Fauvelle, at the same time apologizing for the length of the letter accompanying the poem. He might well have apologized for the length of the poem as well. He must have felt, however vaguely, that his talent did not lie in lengthy, amply developed poems and that such a poem did not correspond to his taste for precision.

The opening of "Les Bois américains" is an evocation of the exotic fauna of the tropical American woods. The sheer abundance of this growth reminds us of some of Chateaubriand's Mississippi landscapes. But above all reminiscences of Leconte de Lisle are evident throughout the poem.[13] The richness and color of tropical growth, the heaviness of natural perfumes, the chorus of birds' songs, the humming of insects, the oppressive heat almost immobilizing physical and mental processes of life — all these elements remind us of Leconte de Lisle's tropical landscapes. Even some of the vocabulary and some of the images are the same, as for example, that of the sun kissing the earth with fiery lips.

Some of the elements found in Romantic poetry earlier in the century are present as well. The third stanza, for example, is devoted largely to a direct statement, although not in the first person, concerning the pleasure of dreaming in solitude amid such tropical splendor, forgetting to turn the pages of the book the speaker has brought along:

> Alors, étendu sous un toit de branches vertes,
> Et regardant sans voir les pages entr'ouvertes,
> Que c'est bon de rêver, solitaire, au doux bruit
> De la source qui pleure un éternel ennui;
> De se sentir à l'ombre et de laisser les rêves
> Printaniers s'élever avec l'odeur des sèves![14]

Then, stretched out beneath the green branches and gazing without seeing the opened pages, how good it is to dream, alone, to the gentle music of the spring which laments an eternal grief, to feel oneself in the cool shade and to let spring dreams rise with the fragrance of the sap.

Another poem written in Cuba is dated Fortuna, October 4, 1860. In a letter of October 27, the same year, Heredia casts some light on the probable circumstances inspiring the poem.[15] The letter is addressed to the Abbé Lefranc, one of Heredia's teachers at Saint-Vincent, a man whom Heredia seems to have held in high esteem and whom he took into his confidence. We learn from the letter that, while at Saint-Vincent, Heredia had become sentimentally attached to a girl whom we can identify only as Geneviève de W. . . . Apparently in an earlier letter the Abbé Lefranc had disillusioned him by some negative remarks about her. Heredia of course was not willing so easily to abandon his illusions, stating that he kept in the depths of his heart a "pure and eternal memory" of his friendship with the girl. With his letter he enclosed the poem referred to above, as a partial reply to the Abbé's letter, adding that in spite of some slight poetic exaggeration everything in the poem is true.

The poem itself recalls the happiness of a summer night in the company of the loved one. There is little in it that prefigures Heredia's mature work. Readers of *Les Trophées* could be forgiven for thinking that this poem had not been written by the same person. It is not sufficient to say that it suggests certain earlier French Romantic poems; what has been borrowed from them is unusually obvious. The first four of its eleven stanzas imitate closely the situation and even the language of Musset's "Lucie," while much of the rest of the poem is based on Musset's "Etoile du soir." Heredia does not conceal his debt, however. Not only does he apostrophize Musset, but he puts into the voice of the beloved several verses from "Etoile du soir." Traces of Lamartine are present in her voice as well. Like that poet's Elvire, she would wish that time would "suspend its flight." Echoes of Hugo's "Tristesse d'Olympio" can also be detected.

VI   *La Conférence La Bruyère*

Heredia's earliest poems thus appear to have been influenced in large part by his reading of the Romantics and Leconte de Lisle. The former he was to leave behind; the latter was eventually to exert an ever increasing influence on him. So far he had not had the benefit of personal contact with other poets or groups of poets. But such contact began very soon after his return to France in 1861.

Beginning around 1850, a number of clubs or associations had been formed in connection with the Faculty of Law in Paris. One of the more long-lived of these was the Conférence La Bruyère, dating from about 1855 and lasting until the mid 1860's. Its purpose was to study and discuss questions of literature, art and philosophy in order to admire the beautiful, seek the true and respect the good.[16] To avoid violent disagreement, discussion of political and religious issues was prohibited. The intellectual activity of the club was thus channeled toward matters relating to history, philosophy, literature and art. It was a closed society organized along strict lines, including a president, two vice-presidents and two secretaries. Entry into the club was difficult; in order to be admitted an applicant had to have three sponsors, be voted in by the membership, and present a poem or some work on an intellectual topic. Annually the society closed its activities with a banquet and issued a bulletin containing the year's contributions by the members.

Heredia joined this society in January, 1862. His name is listed as Joseph de Heredia, a form he had used as a student at Senlis also. Among its members he met a number of poets. His association with at least three of these — Georges Lafenestre, Emmanuel des Essarts and Sully-Prudhomme — was to continue long after his law studies had ended and the Conférence La Bruyère had been disbanded. Of the three, Lafenestre was the oldest and in a sense the leader. He had joined the society in 1856 and had introduced Sully-Prudhomme in 1861. Des Essarts was not a regular member, but as a "corresponding" member he was entitled to publish in the bulletin. It may very well have been these three who sponsored Heredia. In any event he now had an opportunity to mingle with other young poets and to present some of his own verse. To the 1861-2 bulletin he contributed two sonnets ("La Mort d'Agamemnon" and "L'Héliotrope") and five other poems ("Nuit d'été," "Mars," "Ballade sentimentale," "Chanson" and "Coucher de soleil"), while the following year he published one poem ("Mer montante"). The next two bulletins did not contain any of his poetry but the minutes of one of the 1864 meetings indicate that some of his verse had been read and that the question of "Art for art's sake" had been debated by the society.

The character of the poems Heredia contributed to the bulletin of the Conférence La Bruyère did not differ greatly from that of his earlier poems. He was after all only twenty or twenty-one and very little time had elapsed since those early poems. Except for the two sonnets "La Mort d'Agamemnon" and "Mer montante," the dominant theme of the Conférence La Bruyère poems is love. Although the inspiration for most of them seems to have come from his mysterious attachment at Saint-Vincent, one of their striking features is their variety, especially of tone. "La Nuit d'été" and above all "Chanson" evoke a pure, delicate and virginal love in a

paradisiacal setting recalling some of Leconte de Lisle's poems.
"Mars" laments the brevity of time and contains, admittedly expressed with less grace, the Ronsardian admonition to lovers to take
advantage of time while their age is in bloom in its spring season.
"Ballade sentimentale," vaguely reminiscent of Baudelaire's
"Spleen IV" and of certain passages of Verlaine, creates a desolate,
rainy landscape paralleling the gloom of the speaker's soul.
"Coucher de soleil" puts love on a more universal plane; it evokes
the magic of evening in a world where all things seem to unite and
have but one soul and that soul is filled with love. "L'Héliotrope" is
an impersonal love poem in which symbols are the language of love
— the sun, for example, is the "burning lover" kissing the
heliotrope.

Perhaps the price of variety is unevenness. Heredia appears to be
experimenting, possibly looking for a model. Should he be writing
lyric poetry or epic poetry? If lyric, should it be personal or impersonal? If personal, ought he to look to Musset, Lamartine or Ronsard
as his master? Traces of such indecision are present in these poems.
Their sense of unity is sometimes marred by passages borrowed from
other poets and neither disguised nor successfully integrated into his
own inventions.

And yet several possible trends appear to be emerging. First, he is
becoming a little more aware of the importance of workmanship.
"Coucher de soleil," for example, is little more than a reworking of
the earlier "Bois américains," but he has given it a new beginning,
tightened up some of the verses, and supplied a more effective ending. In the second place, he is learning that poetic beauty can result
from a more impersonal approach than that of some of the Romantic
poems he had been reading and, for that matter, writing as well.
Finally, the two sonnets "La Mort d'Agamemnon" and "Mer montante" could be regarded as attempts to leave the love lyric in favor
of a direction more closely resembling the epic approach, whether in
the realm of myth or of nature in its more cosmic manifestations. He
was, in fact, to follow all three of these trends further.

CHAPTER 2

The Poetic Climate

IT was becoming clear that Heredia would devote his life
to poetry. But before following his development further,
let us try to catch some glimpse of his literary milieu, its foremost
personalities, its changing alignments, its dominant poetic theories
and the forces opposed to them. Perhaps it is a commonplace to say
that the evolution of a poet cannot be studied in isolation from the
poetic currents of his time, but it bears repeating because Heredia's
age was one in which poets and other artists in Paris were
remarkably active in the discussion of theories of art and questions of
the day, in the formation of associations, clubs and salons, and in the
founding of journals and reviews. This dynamic and vibrant literary
world into which Heredia was about to find his way was somewhat
like a stage peopled by numerous actors, many of whom played first
one role and then another, while others retained very nearly the
same role from beginning to end.

I *The Romantic Legacy*

From the discussion of Heredia's earliest poems we can see that
aside from Ronsard, the poets whose stamp is most noticeable in
them are Lamartine, Hugo and Musset, or in other words, three of
the four great Romantic poets of the first half of the nineteenth century in France, the fourth being Vigny. Heredia's case was typical
rather than exceptional. These poets left their mark on the early
work of many poets of the second half of the century. Romantic
poetry was their heritage. Their problem was to decide what to do
with it, to what extent to accept, reject, modify or replace it.

The four best-known French Romantic poets still made their
presence felt in varying degrees. The oldest of them, Lamartine,
whose *Méditations poétiques* of 1820 had been such a brilliant
success and, as it were, signaled the renaissance of lyric poetry in the

nineteenth century, had lost much of his prestige by 1860. Memories of his accomplishments as a political figure were fading. He was publishing almost no more poetry. Instead he was putting out a *Cours familier de littérature*, a monthly journal whose literary qualities were not always of the highest. While many poets of the 1860's recognized Lamartine's talent, they objected to his lack of discipline and respect for his art. Although the ethereal fluidity of some of his musical poetry was recaptured by at least one of these poets, Verlaine, a general opposition was growing to what was regarded as Lamartine's basic conception of poetry as a direct and unmuted confession, usually declamatory, of the poet's emotions. The noble ideals and sometime sublimity of his poetry were not enough to save him. Furthermore, the public was tiring of his complaints about his finances as a way of courting public attention.

Of the four, Vigny was perhaps least known by the young poets of the 1860's. Between 1860 and his death in 1863 none of his poetry appeared in the journals of the time. His *Destinées* were published posthumously in 1864. But even during his best years, he was probably not as well known as the other three. He lacked the personal charm of Musset, and he had failed to make a place for himself in public life as Hugo and Lamartine had done. On the other hand, some of those who knew his work well in the 1860's admired certain aspects not only of it but also of the poet's attitude. Some of them, notably Leconte de Lisle, approved of a certain haughty reserve, lacking in the three other famous poets, which led to a less personal and confessional poetic expression. Vigny's aristocratic conception of the poet's status also found favor. He was uncompromising in his refusal to seek personal popularity or to court the approval of the masses by lowering his standards. Furthermore, Leconte de Lisle and Heredia, among others, found in Vigny a link with antiquity by way of André Chénier, from whom Vigny had inherited a love for the past and certain forms and subjects, although it must be added that Vigny's antiquity was chiefly Biblical rather than classical.

It would be difficult to imagine that any French poet of the second half of the nineteenth century could have escaped Victor Hugo's influence. Musset had died before 1860, Vigny and Lamartine during the 1860's, but Hugo lived until 1885. The span of his life thus encompassed all the major poetic movements of the century. His own work continued to be published and republished. Its scope was so vast and so varied that it contained something for almost everyone. During the 1860's his *William Shakespeare, Les*

Misérables and *Chansons des rues et des bois* appeared. In the last two of these alone there was enough to satisfy both those who looked for social and political significance in a piece of writing and those who regarded writing primarily as the art of words.

As a public figure Hugo had not lost any glory; instead, as an exile he had, if anything, added to his celebrity. In that role he seemed to many to be the champion of the downtrodden. The prestige of his poetry was undiminished also. Its power, richness, color, imagery, vision and sheer abundance caused him to be regarded almost with awe as the verbal creator most closely rivaling God. His virtuosity was unmatched. The attitude of many writers toward him was akin to veneration and few dared to make pronouncements of a negative character about him in public. It is true that some poets had reservations about him. They recognized the unevenness of his work and objected to pompous oratory. From the abundance which provided something for every taste one could hardly expect a uniformly lofty standard to be maintained in all its parts. But, in fact, Hugo's separation from others through his exile helped to lend him a certain aura, almost a mythic character, which might have been dispelled through the kind of personal contact known by most other French poets of the 1860's.

We have seen already that Heredia's earliest love poetry owed much to Musset. Musset, who died in 1857, was apparently quite popular with the younger poets of the 1860's. There were those believers in the gospel of social and political relevance in the arts who reproached Musset for being apolitical. Furthermore, his basic approach to poetry as a spontaneous direct expression of the heart was far removed from the doctrine which was widely accepted in the 1860's by a group of poets to which Heredia himself belonged. In spite of this, young poets often made their debut by writing poetry with a Musset flavor. Perhaps he had never really grown up himself. He represented certain qualities with which the young could identify, such as spontaneity, lack of pretentiousness, and above all a direct and ardent sincerity. Possibly he was more liked as a person than admired as an artist. In the three older Romantics the public had discerned some desire for personal aggrandizement, or at least some concern with the image they were projecting. The latter was true even for Vigny. With Musset, however, there appeared to be no pose. He was not ambitious, nor proud, nor calculating. He was, in short, intensely human with his suffering, his weaknesses and even his ability to make fun of himself. As one recent critic puts it, he was the personification of helplessness in the presence of modern tragic destiny.[1]

I should like to add a word about a fifth poet, Gérard de Nerval. Born in 1808, he was a slightly younger contemporary of the other four Romantics. Steeped in German culture, he showed strong affinities with German Romanticism. His poetic universe, situated largely in the world of dreams, was the setting for his quest of the eternal feminine, which took him back in time to the exploration of various religions and mythologies. This quest was linked also with the search for his own identity, which he pursued in the same domains. He died in 1855. His poetry, so little concerned with material reality and so much an evocation of a profound inner world where feeling, religion, myth and legend often merged, was forward looking, having its main impact after the 1860's.

The five poets to whom I have just referred were all more or less out of circulation by the early 1860's when Heredia finished his education and was ready to find a place among the poets of the day. Nerval and Musset were dead, Hugo was in exile, Vigny died in 1863 and Lamartine held himself aloof from the younger poets.

II   *The Literary Milieu*

Who were these younger poets and what was the nature of the literary scene they were part of in the 1860's? Paris seemed to be full of poets and other artists at this time. Some of the poets — Gautier, Leconte de Lisle, Baudelaire, Banville, for example — were no longer really young and had already published a large part, if not most, of their mature poetry. Many, like Heredia, had been born around 1840. Others were still younger. There was much interaction among them. They met in groups in cafés or in the apartments or homes of some of them. Sometimes groups would form around a literary journal. The composition of a group often changed only slightly according to the meeting place and in some instances not at all.

These poets were of various backgrounds: poor or rich, bourgeois or aristocratic, provincial or Parisian. But they were united in the sense that a generation can be united when confronted by a common problem. There are at least some parallels to be drawn between them and the poets of the 1820's. The earlier poets faced a common problem too: to construct a new set of values in politics, society, religion and art after the French Revolution and the Napoleonic era had effectively put an end to one chapter in history, and opened a new one whose pages were still largely blank. During the 1820's writers also gathered in groups, adhered to journals, took a stand in politics, discussed art, and eventually worked out certain literary ideas common to most of the members and which are sometimes called Romantic doctrine.

Similarly, poets in the decade 1860 to 1870 were trying to define the role of their art in relation to their time. The Revolution of 1848 had disillusioned many of them, and the imperial regime of Louis Napoleon did not conform to the ideal of most of them. Middle-class materialism appeared to be the dominant way of life in France. Christianity seemed to many to be an outworn creed. In spite of its many useful contributions, science revealed the forces of determinism as a modern equivalent of the relentless fate of antiquity, largely beyond man's control. In these circumstances, did man really have any freedom to shape his own destiny? As for the poet, should he still attempt through his art to play a role in politics and society or, other values failing him, should he seek his salvation in the creation of beauty? These were some of the questions with which these poets grappled. Out of their meetings, their discussions and their publications, a common core of ideas began to emerge before the end of the decade. The dominant figure among them was Leconte de Lisle. In spite of the fact that there was much diversity among them, a significant number shared certain basic ideas. Literary history calls them the Parnassian poets.

Before examining the ideas of the Parnassians, I should like to identify and characterize briefly some of the various groupings of the poets of the decade. A number of them met in certain cafés such as the Café Procope, the Café de Madrid, the Café des Variétés and the Brasserie des Martyrs, but much more important meeting places were several salons, usually homes or apartments where hosts received on a regular basis once a week or more often. The activities at these gatherings included poetry readings, discussions, charades, presentations of scenes from plays, outings in summer, theater parties in winter, largely according to the tone set by the host. The most important of these salons were those of Catulle Mendès, the Marquise de Ricard, Leconte de Lisle, Alphonse Lemerre and Nina de Villard.

One of the first of these groups was associated with the *Revue fantaisiste,* founded early in 1861 by Catulle Mendès, who came from a prosperous Bordeaux family. He was about Heredia's age, talented, enterprising and, for a few years, the dominant figure among the

future Parnassians. Many of his guests were contributors to his journal and continued to be involved in his *Revue française*, which
succeeded the short-lived *Revue fantaisiste*. Mendès' role in the
history of the Parnassians was not insignificant. In addition to
supplying a first rallying point with his salon and journal, he continued to support and initiate other journals and publications and
himself left two documents of interest for historians of the Parnassian
group: *La Légende du Parnasse* and *Rapport sur le mouvement
poétique français de 1867 à 1900.*

Another founder of journals was Louis-Xavier de Ricard, a friend
of Mendès and also about the same age. His *Revue du progrès moral,
littéraire, scientifique et artistique*, begun in 1863, was replaced in
1865 by *L'Art*, which formulated some of the poetic doctrines of the
Parnassians. Mendès collaborated with Ricard and in a sense the two
could be regarded as the real founders of the Parnassian group.
Ricard's mother took an interest in her son's friends, and in 1863 she
began opening her doors to them weekly. Her salon, which was in its
heyday between 1865 and 1868, was perhaps less exclusively literary
than that of Mendès and certainly less so than Leconte de Lisle's. Its
atmosphere was relatively gay and easy and its character tended to
become more and more bohemian.

This flavor was continued in 1868 in the salon of Nina de Villard,
the Countess of Callias. She favored poets and received officially on
Wednesdays and Sundays. In actual fact, however, she appears to
have kept virtually an open house nearly all the time for those poets
interested in conversation, charades, eating, or poetry reading.
Perhaps these gatherings became altogether too frivolous; in any
event, some of the more "proper" Parnassians felt the salon was
deteriorating and began to stay away. Nina herself was probably
somewhat unbalanced and to some, at least, she appeared strange.

Leconte de Lisle's salon, on the other hand, was much more sober.
By the mid 1860's he had become a central figure among the poets of
the time and most of them appeared at one time or another at his
weekly Saturday receptions held in his fifth floor apartment at 8
Boulevard des Invalides. They went there, said Heredia, with the
same fervor as Moslems go to Mecca.[2] Madame Leconte de Lisle was
a gracious hostess, but left the center of the stage for her husband.
He was usually stern but kind and encouraging to the young,
sometimes feared, but respected by almost everyone. Conversation
at his salons tended to be serious and elevated. Many poets, especially the younger ones, submitted their verse to him for his judg-

ment and advice, and he read his own poetry in an impressive
manner. A severe critic of himself, he taught a religious respect for
art, disdain of easy success, and nobility of thought.
The years 1851 to 1866 had been difficult ones for those wishing to
publish poetry. Some publishers simply did not accept poetry, and
even Gautier, Banville and Leconte de Lisle at times had difficulty
finding a publisher. This situation was eased somewhat in 1865 when
an eccentric violinist, Ernest Boutier, introduced Ricard to his friend
Alphonse Lemerre, a publisher. This was a valuable connection for
the poets. Before long, daily meetings of poets were taking place in
late afternoon in the entresol of Lemerre's bookshop. Discussions
were often loud and spirited, and customers must sometimes have
wondered what was going on. Lemerre himself continued to support
Ricard's *L'Art*. Soon Ricard and Mendès had the idea of replacing
L'Art with a collection exclusively devoted to poetry, which was to
be a kind of organ or manifesto of the group. They undertook joint
editorship of the collection under the title *Le Parnasse contemporain: recueil de vers nouveaux*. It is not clear who selected the title. Several numbers appeared in 1865, and in 1866 Lemerre undertook to publish the poems in book form. Almost at once the poets
who had participated became known as the Parnassians.[3]
Almost all the well-known living French poets had been invited to
contribute, the only very noticeable absentees being Lamartine and
Hugo. Altogether thirty-seven poets were represented. Financially
the venture was not successful, and only Baudelaire and Leconte de
Lisle were paid for their collaboration. Nor was the poetry contained
in the collection distinguished, on the whole. On the positive side,
however, a large number of poets had found a means of bringing
their poetry in a modest way before the public.
The *Parnasse contemporain* of 1866 was followed by two other
issues, the first of these in 1869 (but not published until 1871 on account of the Franco-Prussian War), and the second in 1876. The *Parnasse contemporain* of 1869 was produced at Lemerre's expense,
who took the initiative in inviting poets to collaborate. It is not clear
who edited this issue, but undoubtedly Leconte de Lisle's influence
was already being strongly felt. This time there were fifty-six contributors, thirty-one of whom had not participated in the first issue.
Some of the weaker poets of the 1866 issue had not been invited, and
all in all the quality of the second issue was better, although it did
not seem to attract as much attention as the first. The third *Parnasse
contemporain* was extremely heterogeneous in character. More than

ixty poets contributed to it, and there were no noticeable principles governing the choice of poems. I think it is safe to suspect that the criteria used to accept or reject contributions were not always literary. After 1870 the group was beginning to disperse. This was especially true of the older poets, who began to frequent the various salons less regularly. The reasons for this dispersal were several in number. The war, growing divergence of ideas, internal dissension, incompatibility of personalities — all these contributed to the dissolution of the group. The feeling of belonging to a group had weakened greatly since the 1860's and many poets were finding other directions further removed from those common to any group. Moreover, by 1876 there was considerable rivalry and jealousy among the poets. It is true that not all salons had closed — Leconte de Lisle, for example, continued to receive some of the old faithful as well as some new ones — but clearly the heyday of the Parnassians was over.

III *The Parnassian School*

It is sometimes contended that the Parnassian poets were never a poetic school but only a loosely associated group of poets sharing several basic ideas about poetry. Some of the poets themselves, notably Mendès, Ricard, des Essarts, Verlaine, Lepelletier, and Coppée, denied that they belonged to a school of poetry, or even that the group had a real leader.[4] Mendès relates an amusing anecdote to explain how the group was formed. According to him, it all began one day when the poet Glatigny brought in his *Vignes folles* for publication in the *Revue fantaisiste*. Mendès having perused the collection, the following scene reportedly took place between them, beginning with an exclamation by Mendès:

"Vous êtes un poète!" . . . Glatigny répliqua: "Vous en êtes un autre!" Ces injures échangées, les deux jeunes gens se serrèrent la main: et ce fut le commencement du groupe qui devait se former.[5]

"You are a poet!" . . . Glatigny replied: "You are one too!" — These insults having been exchanged, the two young men shook hands; and that was the beginning of the group which was to be formed.

Théophile Gautier, on the other hand, saw the Parnassians as a school with an unmistakable leader:

Leconte de Lisle a réuni autour de lui une école, un cénacle, comme vous voudrez l'appeler, de jeunes poètes qui l'admirent avec raison, car il a toutes les hautes qualités d'un chef d'école, et qui l'imitent du mieux qu'ils peuvent, ce dont on les blâme à tort, selon nous, car celui qui n'a pas été disciple ne sera jamais maître.[6]

Leconte de Lisle has gathered around him a school, a cénacle, you might say, of young poets who admire him, with good reason, for he possesses all the high qualities of a school head, and they imitate him as well as they can, for which it is wrong to blame them, in our opinion, for whoever has not been a disciple will never be a master.

From a twentieth-century viewpoint, I think, it is clear that Leconte de Lisle was the dominant figure among the Parnassians. But it is difficult to find any clear-cut manifesto accepted as the literary doctrine of the group, although Leconte de Lisle and a few others did expose their personal poetic creeds. On the whole, the group was not very combative or revolutionary in the sense that the Romantics are sometimes called revolutionary. Whether or not the Parnassians ought to be called a school of poetry is perhaps irrelevant. It is more useful to try to determine which poets belonged to the group and what were the attitudes and ideas about poetry which they held in common.

As we saw earlier, the label "Parnassian" began to be used after the appearance of the first issue of the *Parnasse contemporain* in 1866. It was applied, loosely speaking, to those poets who had contributed to the various issues of that publication. Altogether that amounted to some ninety-five poets, or almost all the "known" French poets of the time. Many of them had little more in common than that they published in the *Parnasse contemporain*. Obviously they were not all Parnassians, if the term was to mean anything at all. However, of this large number only fourteen were represented in all three issues of the *Parnasse:* Banville, Cazalis, Coppée, Dierx, des Essarts, Heredia, Leconte de Lisle, Lemoyne, Mendès, Mérat, Renaud, Ricard, Sully-Prudhomme, Valade. This reduction can be explained in several ways. First, many of the weakest poets had not been invited to contribute a second time, thus leaving a core of some of the better poets. Secondly, a number of the good poets were no longer associated with the common ground of the Parnassians or had for other reasons disappeared from the literary scene. Gautier, for example, had died before the third issue was published. After their brief association with the *Parnasse contemporain*, Verlaine,

Baudelaire and Mallarmé, all first-rate poets, turned in the direction of the Symbolist movement. Perhaps it would be hard to find general agreement as to which poets should be included under the heading "Parnassian," but the fourteen names just listed, with the possible addition of Glatigny and Silvestre, might serve as a useful core, even though such lists almost inevitably have some element of arbitrariness in them. It is well to remember, in any case, that Gautier was their most illustrious precursor and that Baudelaire, Mallarmé and Verlaine had contributed "Parnassian" poetry of merit.

IV   *The Parnassian Ideal*

What was the common literary ground of the Parnassians? Perhaps it would be better to speak of general tendencies, since even in this group there was not complete uniformity of opinion. It may be that what united them most was a conception of poetry which differed in some significant ways from that of the Romantics. A well-known sonnet of Leconte de Lisle, entitled "Les Montreurs" (The Showmen), is a convenient starting point for an explanation of some of these differences. The two quatrains which open the poem present images of undignified display. The parading of a bleak, bruised and dust-covered animal by a showman before a vulgar public, or the immodest act of disrobing to provide the spectators a cheap thrill, corresponds to some poets' display of their own heart. The sonnet ends with the following sestet:

> Dans mon orgueil muet, dans ma tombe sans gloire,
> Dussé-je m'engloutir pour l'éternité noire,
> Je ne te vendrai pas mon ivresse ou mon mal,
>
> Je ne livrerai pas ma vie à tes huées,
> Je ne danserai pas sur ton tréteau banal
> Avec tes histrions et tes prostituées.

In my mute pride, in my grave without glory, if I should be engulfed for all of dark eternity, I shall not sell you my ecstasies or my pain, I shall not deliver my life to your jeers, I shall not dance on your vulgar stage with your histrions and your prostitutes.

In this sonnet Leconte de Lisle condemns first of all the practice, often followed by Romantic poets, of expressing directly their personal feelings and thus in a sense putting their hearts on public display. The Romantics were not always guilty of this practice. Vigny, for example, tended to be much more impersonal than the others, finding ways of communicating his feelings through symbolic characters. Perhaps because of the strong reaction expressed by Leconte de Lisle and shared by his comrades, the Parnassians came to be regarded as impassive. It is not clear how the term began to be applied to them. Glatigny had written a play entitled *L'Impassible*, and Gautier had contributed a sonnet, "L'Impassible," to the second *Parnasse contemporain*. Apparently the term had also been attributed to Leconte de Lisle even before 1866. On the other hand, Xavier de Ricard claimed credit for having been the first to call the group "Les Impassibles" (The Impassive Ones). But in fact the term "impassive" is a misnomer and most of the Parnassians would not have applied it to themselves. Perhaps Leconte de Lisle's views on the subject are typical. In any case they are unequivocal:

En aura-t-on bientôt fini avec cette baliverne! Poète impassible! Alors quand on ne raconte pas de quelle façon on boutonne son pantalon, et les péripéties de ses amourettes, on est un poète impassible? C'est stupide.[7]

Will we never hear the last of such rubbish! Impassive poet indeed! If you don't relate how you button your trousers, and all the ups and downs of every little love affair, you're an impassive poet? That's silly!

The truth is that the Parnassians did not systematically refrain from expressing personal emotion. Rather they reacted against the unrestrained confessional poetry of the Romantics, which was too lyrically expansive, impassioned and oratorical.

Another idea that is expressed in "Les Montreurs" is that the poet is in a sense an elitist. Poetry is not for the masses; its appeal should never be to the vulgar. The poet must not lower his lofty standards of beauty to gain the favor of the multitudes, thereby debasing himself and his art and descending to the level of a prostitute and cheap entertainer. Perhaps the greatest legacy Leconte de Lisle left to those whom he influenced was a high respect for art and beauty and for the discipline required to produce formal perfection.

The cult of beauty and perfection of form was, in fact, a major concern among the Parnassians. It was for them the chief *raison d'être* of poetry. Its purpose, in their view, was not primarily to express the emotions of the heart, to serve social causes, to present moral teaching, nor even to seek the truth; it was simply to create beauty. Beauty was the summit, the point of convergence of man's intellectual activity. Since it was its own final goal it could serve no master. This conception is, of course, that of art for art's sake, and the Parnassians were not the first nineteenth-century French poets to speak of it. Victor Hugo in his 1829 preface to *Les Orientales* refers to the collection as a useless book of pure poetry thrown out into the midst of grave public preoccupations. But it was Gautier who had stated the principle of art for art's sake most forcefully.

It was Gautier also in the well-known poem "L'Art" who characterized the Parnassian ideal of formal beauty by comparing poetry to the plastic arts of painting and especially sculpture. Gautier and Leconte de Lisle both emphasized the necessity of discipline and hard work as against the apparently uncontrolled spontaneity of some Romantic poetry. Gautier viewed the poet's struggle with language as no less difficult than that of the sculptor with the hardness of his stone. A mastery of technique was therefore essential to achieve perfection of form. Perhaps Banville more than any other Parnassian occupied himself with questions of technique and, as a technical virtuoso, was an authority in these matters for the group, even publishing a treatise, in 1872, on French poetry. It was he especially who set forth the importance of rich rhyme, stating that rhyme is the only generator of French verse. In general, however, the Parnassians did not introduce many innovations into French versification: instead, they insisted on greater mastery of it.

Gautier was a man "for whom the visible world existed." Many other Parnassians could have said the same thing. Poetry based on a conception similar to that of sculpture and painting presupposes an interest in objects. Furthermore, the presentation of objects, of aspects of the visible world, was an alternative to lyrical expansiveness, one way of being more impersonal and objective. Much Parnassian poetry thus tended to be labeled "descriptive." Its readers can find in it descriptions of animals, landscapes, flowers, inanimate objects, and even scenes from everyday life. The best of these descriptions are unforgettable and symbolical; however, in the hands of second-rate poets the result is often mere photographic transcription.

Another important tendency of Parnassian poetry was the resurrection of the past. *Parnasse* (Parnassus) itself, as the name of the mountain which was the legendary abode of Apollo and the Muses, evokes memories of Ancient Greece. The erudition and documentation which made possible the evocation of the past owed no small debt to the enormous strides made during the nineteenth century in the development of history as a discipline. The historical era preferred by many of the Parnassians was classical Greece, no doubt because that period corresponded so closely to their own ideal of beauty. But many other historical epochs, from the prehistoric to the present, attracted their attention as well. The resurrection of the past was inspired not only by history but also by legend and mythology. A number of Parnassians, for example, explored various religions in their poetry. Perhaps the present was felt by some of the poets to be too objectionable and too unbearable. That is how Leconte de Lisle felt. Perhaps the past allowed a more objective perspective. Perhaps also it held valuable keys to the understanding of the most fundamental problems of being. Finally, perhaps the past was felt, as it had been by the Romantics, to have been more poetic than the present.

Most of the Parnassian ideals had in fact already existed earlier, even among the Romantics. Isolated descriptions of animals can be found even in Musset, target of so much Parnassian criticism. Vigny's reserve and reluctance to be too personal have already been mentioned. Interest in the past, in antiquity, in religions, and in a kind of epic of man can be seen in all four major French Romantic poets. We need only think of Hugo's *Légende des siècles*, of Lamartine's evocation of the primitive ages of man in *La Chute d'un ange* (which Leconte de Lisle and Heredia both admired), of Vigny's choice of subjects from classical and Biblical antiquity, and even of Musset, who invokes Greece, "mother of the arts," and joins with the Parnassians in finding beauty in the religion of antiquity. But with the Parnassians these tendencies were much more pronounced and occupied a central position in their poetics. It is thus largely a question of degree and proportion. Perhaps it is accurate to say that, in general, the Parnassians were not so much an innovative group but rather a later stage in the development of Romanticism.

CHAPTER 3

Heredia and the Parnassians

I have tried in the preceding chapter to present some notion of the social and literary milieu in which Heredia found himself at the time when he was completing his formal education. It will be remembered that the Conférence La Bruyère, which Heredia joined in 1862, already included the poets Georges Lafenestre, Emmanuel des Essarts and Sully-Prudhomme. All three were closely associated with the Parnassians. Des Essarts and Sully-Prudhomme, like Heredia himself, later contributed to all three issues of the *Parnasse contemporain*.

Georges Lafenestre was perhaps the first of Heredia's Parnassian friends. One of the oldest members of the Conférence La Bruyère, he was also one of its most active and faithful members. Although he lacked the talent to be a great writer, he contributed to a number of reviews. As a man he was respected and liked; his social graces, ease of manner, serenity, pleasant smile, cordiality and genuine modesty made him popular, especially in Leconte de Lisle's salon, which he preferred to those of Mendès and Ricard. He was, in fact, one of the first to go to Leconte de Lisle's salon and he succeeded in winning the host's esteem. The friendship between Lafenestre and Heredia was a durable one. It is probable that Lafenestre not only supported Heredia as a candidate for the Conférence La Bruyère but also facilitated his further contact with other poets. As an indication of deepening friendship, the two poets took a trip to Italy together in 1864 and for many years carried on a correspondence in which Heredia often confided in his friend.

I *The Man Heredia*

During the 1860's and later, Heredia had many other friends and cordial acquaintances. Both his appearance and personality were attractive, and he appeared to have a gift for making friends. In her letters to Fauvelle during José-Maria's school days, Madame Heredia more than once notes a resemblance between her son and her husband, as when she speaks of his strong and masculine handsomeness. Several verbal portraits of him were composed by his contemporaries. Coppée, for example, describes him as follows:

> ... un beau créole de la Havane, très brun, tête rase et barbe frisée, le premier ciseleur de sonnets de ce temps-ci, qui compte parmi ses ancêtres un Grand Inquisiteur et l'un des intrépides compagnons de Cortez, le "Conquistador."[1]

> ... a handsome Creole from Havana, very dark, hair cropped and wavy beard, the leading sculptor of sonnets of this period, who counts among his ancestors a Grand Inquisitor and one of the intrepid companions of Cortes, the "Conquistador."

As if to confirm the last part of the statement Claudius Popelin, an enameler and friend of Heredia and the Parnassians, made a portrait showing Heredia in the costume of a *conquistador*.

This image of the *conquistador* was evoked not only by his ancestry but also by a certain elegance and aristocratic distinction in his bearing, manners and tastes. His ideal was that of the well-rounded and cultivated man. His suits were impeccably cut and, according to Anatole France, his ties were as striking as his sonnets.[2] Perhaps he was even a little vain about his concept of the gentleman — some of his eulogies of others would end with the words, "And besides, he is a gentleman." But on the whole, moderation was one of his greatest virtues. He was not one normally to bear grudges and, where many would have been envious, he was generous. Although there was a great deal of jealousy among the Parnassians, Heredia was able to remain on good terms with almost all of them. He had no taste for literary disputes, fame or public approval. Unlike many of his comrades, young like himself, he was not radical or hypercritical. Like most of them he disapproved of the imperial regime of his time, but in general held an aversion to politics.

Socially Heredia must have been very pleasant. Simple and easy in manner, he was always cordial and affable, treating every one alike, whether he be a celebrity or a neophyte. Although he was sincere and often frank, he possessed the unusual virtue of not denigrating any one. Inclined to be talkative, he was usually in the forefront of conversation, enthusiastic, exuberant and spontaneous, constantly lighting his pipe or smoking a cigar, a habit which his mother had hoped he would abandon. He liked telling anecdotes and was not without a sense of humor. He was interested in almost every subject and every person and responded easily, his speech colorful and accompanied by suitable gestures. Perhaps one of his most striking features was his voice, strong and sonorous and with some of the mellow quality of a brass instrument. Heredia had a slight speech impediment, a kind of stutter or hesitation; but instead of causing him to repeat syllables, it made him rather prolong them in such a way that it added a peculiar charm and dramatic effect to his speech and poetry reading.

Heredia tended to be discriminating with regard to the salons and cafés he frequented. He would go to the Café Voltaire, for example, but not to Montmartre when the group met there. He was, of course, an *habitué* of Leconte de Lisle's salon but went only on rare occasions to the more frivolous gatherings of Nina de Villard. He also went to the more aristocratic salons of the Princess Mathilde and broadened his literary contacts by going beyond the immediate Parnassian group to the salons of Daudet and the Goncourt brothers, as well as seeing something of Taine.

II *Friendships*

Heredia soon became well known in literary circles, and he appears to have been acquainted with almost all the French writers of any consequence who were his contemporaries. He even had occasion to meet Lamartine and Hugo. His admiration for the former dated from childhood and when he finally saw him for the first time he stood almost in awe as if he were in the presence of a god.[3] Heredia's first chance to meet Hugo did not come until after the latter's return to France from exile, when many of his compatriots hastened to pay their respects to the great poet. Heredia, whose feelings for Hugo came close to veneration, was not disappointed by the warm reception and cordial chat he enjoyed during his visit.[4] In 1902 he had the honor of presiding at the commemoration of Hugo's centenary held at the Sorbonne.

Relations between Heredia and Gautier were notably cordial. Heredia admired the latter's work, and Gautier took an immediate liking to Heredia, addressing him as early as their first meeting by the familiar pronoun "tu." With disarming directness and simplicity he told Heredia he liked him and his heroic and sonorous name.[5] Gautier seems to have taken some delight in a little good-humored teasing: when Heredia contributed a few sonnets to the *Revue française* in 1863, Gautier is said to have exclaimed: "Comment! Si jeune, et tu fais déjà des sonnets libertins!"[6] [What! So young and you are already producing libertine sonnets!]

Another of his older contemporaries whose friendship he enjoyed particularly was Théodore de Banville. The latter had a special affection for Heredia and Coppée, who both took pleasure in going to Banville's famous dinners. Although Banville did not possess the qualities of a leader, his devotion to his poetic craft and his theories concerning it nonetheless commanded Heredia's respect and contributed not a little to his apprenticeship. In a letter to Coppée, dated February 17, 1892, he pays this tribute to Banville:

Banville a été pour nous tous, cher ami, un maître fraternel. J'ai toujours eu pour lui beaucoup d'admiration, une réelle affection, un vrai respect. Il a été le plus parfait des littérateurs, le plus scrupuleux des écrivains.[7]

Banville, my dear friend, was for all of us a fraternal master. I have always had much admiration, real affection and true respect for him. He was the most perfect of literary men, the most scrupulous of writers.

Several other friendships are worth singling out. A mutual admiration existed between Heredia and Flaubert. Heredia rarely missed Flaubert's Sunday receptions in Paris and sometimes visited the novelist at Croisset. Flaubert, for his part, admired Heredia's prose and wrote him brief but cordial notes. François Coppée, about the same age as Heredia, enjoyed a long friendship with him. Paul Verlaine, whom he often took to Banville's dinners, considered him a friend all his life and dedicated a number of poems to him. Even the eccentric Villiers de l'Isle Adam, chronically short of money, felt the hand of Heredia's friendship, a hand that extended loans which were seldom repaid on time.

The cordial relations which Heredia was able to establish and maintain with his contemporaries had but few exceptions. Perhaps the most notable of these was Baudelaire. Heredia recalls that upon being presented to that poet he tried respectfully to express his admiration for his *Fleurs du mal*. Baudelaire, staring at him coldly, interrupted him with the words, "Monsieur, je n'aime pas les jeunes gens" [Sir, I do not like young people], and then turned his back.[8] Although Heredia continued to admire Baudelaire's poetry, he could never quite forgive the poet. There were some awkward moments between Heredia and Anatole France as well. On one occasion he asked the latter, imprudently perhaps, to sign a manifesto stating Victor Hugo to be the greatest French poet. France was prepared to concede that Hugo was great but not the greatest. His refusal to sign led to bitter words between the two.[9] But Heredia's sense of tact usually helped him avoid unpleasant clashes, especially on controversial subjects. On one occasion Louis Ménard, the celebrated and erudite hellenist from whom Heredia obtained an appreciation of the nature of true hellenism and of the distinction between Greek and Latin theogony, proposed sacrificing some doves to Venus. Heredia, who was Catholic, did not wish to push his hellenism that far and extricated himself gracefully by declaring that he was not fond of pigeon.[10]

III   *Heredia and Leconte de Lisle*

Of all Heredia's friendships, the one with Leconte de Lisle was by far the most remarkable. It will be recalled that his first acquaintance with the older man was through the latter's poetry at the time of Heredia's graduation from Saint-Vincent. Their first meeting face to face took place in 1863 in Heredia's apartment in the rue de Tournon, where he then lived with his mother, who generously invited her son's friends and occasionally helped them financially. For Heredia, Leconte de Lisle was not only a friend but also a teacher and a counselor. It became clear to all that Heredia was the older poet's favorite disciple.

There were some obvious parallels between them. Both were Creoles. Both had come from a tropical island, grown up on a plantation, gone to France at an early age to be educated, come back to their island briefly and returned to France for the rest of their lives. And both could claim some Norman ancestry. On the other hand, Heredia was twenty-four years younger than Leconte de Lisle and their temperaments differed markedly. Whereas Heredia was optimistic, often gay, and generally moderate, Leconte de Lisle tended to be pessimistic and grave. Perhaps the differences between them also helped to hold them together. Their contrasting temperaments may well have served as mutually corrective influences and the difference in age made the master-disciple relationship easier. It is tempting to theorize that Heredia looked upon Leconte de Lisle as he might have regarded his own father, whom he had lost so early in life. In fact he referred to Leconte de Lisle as "my master," "a parent" (or relative) and "a great older brother."

As time passed it became more and more apparent that Leconte de Lisle regarded the Heredias as something more than friends. In March, 1867, José-Maria had married the sixteen-year-old Louise Despaigne from Nantes. She was from a family originally transplanted to Cuba and already allied to the Heredias since 1858, when José-Maria's sister had married Louis Despaigne. In 1871 the first of three daughters was born to José-Maria and his wife at Menton. The names of the three were Hélène, Marie and Louise.[11] The family often took vacations near the Pyrenees, or, more rarely, in Normandy. Leconte de Lisle would sometimes be invited to spend a few weeks with the Heredias at these times. The family treated him with affection and the girls regarded him as a grandfather, a role he did not mind playing. He must have taken comfort in the strength and concern of his younger friend, a concern even expressed occasionally in terms of financial assistance.

Apart from these personal ties it is clear that a considerable community of mind and artistic outlook, not to mention high mutual professional esteem, existed between the two men. As early as 1863 Heredia dedicated his sonnet "Le Triomphe d'Iaccos," published in the *Revue française*, to Leconte de Lisle. The two men read each other's poetry, consulted each other before publishing it and encouraged each other. Heredia paid the following tribute to his master for the debt he and others owed him:

Leconte de Lisle! Mais il nous a appris à tous à faire des vers! et les conseils qu'il nous donnait ce n'était pas du tout pour que nous fassions des vers comme les siens, il se mettait dans la peau de chacun: "Moi, à votre place, je mettrais ceci, je changerais cela." Et gaiement, fraternellement! Oui, nous devons tous le respecter, le vénérer, l'aimer comme il nous a aimés, d'une grande affection dévouée . . . — Par son illustre exemple plus encore que par ses conseils, il nous a enseigné le respect de la noble langue française, l'amour désintéressé de la poésie. Nous lui devons la conscience de notre art.[12]

Leconte de Lisle! Why he taught us all to write verse! And the advice he gave us was not at all intended to make us write verse like his. He would put himself in each person's place: "If I were you I should put this, I should change that." And cheerfully, fraternally! Yes, we must all respect, venerate and love him as he loved us . . . — By his illustrious example, even more than by his advice, he taught us respect for the noble French language and unselfish love of poetry. We owe to him our awareness of our art.

In Heredia's art as well as in his personal life, then, it seems that

Leconte de Lisle played a father role, watching his poems being born one by one. In a very real sense he was a teacher. His advice was not limited to generalities; he criticized details in his disciple's poems and provided advice to correct errors.[13] Heredia respected these corrections and was intelligent enough to profit from them. The criticisms were not all negative. Leconte de Lisle was happy to express his admiration of what he found good and declared that the French language had never reached a greater degree of perfection than in Heredia's poetry.[14]

Leconte de Lisle had the good fortune to live long enough to witness the fulfillment of some of Heredia's aspirations. The publication of *Les Trophées* in 1893 must have given him a sense of accomplishment not only for his disciple but also for himself. On February 22, 1894, Leconte de Lisle enjoyed another of Heredia's successes, when the latter, competing against Zola, Verlaine and two lesser figures, was elected to the Académie Française. Unfortunately death claimed the aging poet on July 17, 1894, and deprived him of the pleasure of attending Heredia's reception at the French Academy on May 30, 1895. It was fitting that it was Heredia who gave the funeral oration for him at Saint-Sulpice. This final tribute not only expressed his high esteem but also summarized with characteristic succinctness and precision the nature of Leconte de Lisle's poetry:

. . . il a suscité devant nous les dieux, les races, les civilisations disparues, les bêtes sauvages, les pays lointains. En des vers d'une beauté sereine et tragique, il a traduit le tumulte des passions, l'éternel désir, les révoltes de la raison et de l'orgueil, l'angoisse du désespoir, ce que l'amour et la foi ont de plus féroce et de plus suave, toute l'âme antique, toute l'âme moderne, l'humanité.[15]

. . . he has resurrected before our eyes gods, races, extinct civilizations, wild animals, distant lands. In verses of serene or tragic beauty he has translated the tumult of passions, eternal desire, the revolt of reason and pride, the anguish of despair, the sweetness and the ferocity of love and faith, the whole soul of antiquity, the whole modern soul, humanity.

Later Heredia was to unveil a bust of Leconte de Lisle in the Luxembourg Gardens, where, incidentally, there is now also a bust of Heredia. It was entirely fitting, also, that for his reception speech at the French Academy, he wore with pride Leconte de Lisle's academician's sword as well as his green academician's gown, the

latter having been given to him by Madame Leconte de Lisle in
memory of her husband. Clearly Leconte de Lisle had picked
Heredia as his successor, and the sword which had passed on to him
seemed a symbolic bequest.

IV *Heredia's Salons*

Although Heredia liked being with people, he preferred the role
of host to that of guest. During the early 1860's his mother would in-
vite some of his friends from time to time to their apartment on rue
de Tournon. But it was not until after his marriage in 1867 that he
began receiving on a regular basis, on Thursdays. After moving first
to the avenue de Breteuil and then to the rue de Berri, the Heredias
settled in a large apartment on the rue Balzac in 1885. Here the
reception day was changed to Saturday. By this time Leconte
de Lisle was nearing seventy and in a sense Heredia's "Saturdays"
replaced or perhaps continued Leconte de Lisle's "Saturdays."
    These receptions usually began at three o'clock in the afternoon.
The guests were numerous. The former *habitués* of Leconte de
Lisle's salon now also came to Heredia's receptions. Some of the
writers of the time who were among the guests were: Leconte
de Lisle, Sully-Prudhomme, Cazalis, Léon Barracand, André
Theuriet, Jules Breton, Henry Bordeaux, Henri de Régnier, le
vicomte de Guerne, Maurice Maindron, Emile Pouvillon, Edmond
Biré, Paul Hervieu, Georges de Porto-Riche, Louis Bertrand, Jean
Psichari, Gaston Deschamps, Albert Samain, Pierre Louÿs, A.-F.
Herold, Robert de Bonnières, Henri Mazel, le vicomte d'Avenel,
Charles Le Goffic, Robert de Sizeranne, Marcel Schwob, Maxime
Formont, Alfred Poizat, Fernand Gregh, Auguste Angellier, and
J. C. Mardrus.[16] In addition, there were celebrities other than
writers; in fact, these receptions gathered together the most distinguished intellectuals, artists and diplomats in Paris.
    In 1901, when he was named administrator of the Bibliothèque de
l'Arsenal, perhaps the most literary of libraries, Heredia moved
again and changed with the Saturday receptions to Sunday. He was
happy with the post. Perhaps it was a kind of sinecure. He devoted
only a short time each day to it, except for Thursdays, which were reserved for the Academy. But he was a conscientious administrator,
sent numerous reports to the Ministry of Education, renovated, organized displays, purchased manuscripts and obtained donated collections.
    By this time he was writing less and less, and had ample time to

receive. He was an admirable host, less masterful but more gracious than Leconte de Lisle. The atmosphere of his "Sundays" was pleasant. Heredia's love of beauty was evident even in the statuettes, pictures and knick-knacks with which he had surrounded himself. Popelin's enamel portrait of Heredia as a *conquistador* was proudly displayed in the salon. Conversation was lively in the smoke-filled room. Socially Heredia was animated, often spoke in superlatives and was a lover of anecdotes. He circulated among his guests, speaking in his cordial and sincere way to each one, celebrity or beginner, putting each one at ease. To new-comers he was especially kind and attentive, giving generously of his advice and helping more than one of them find a publisher.

Undoubtedly Heredia was aware of the fact that a little more than seventy years earlier the Bibliothèque de l'Arsenal had been the center of the best-known French Romantic salon, when Nodier was the librarian. Now the Romantics had been replaced by the Parnassians. And yet that was no longer strictly true either. By 1901 the guest list had changed considerably from that of the 1860's. The high point of the Parnassians had passed and the Symbolists had for some years been the reigning poetic school. But even during his "Saturdays" Heredia had welcomed Symbolist poets to his receptions. It is true that the Symbolists attacked Parnassian doctrine and it is equally true that Heredia had reservations about Symbolist free verse. He could not understand why they called themselves Symbolists in the first place, since all good poets, he felt, were symbolists.[17] In any case, there had always been a good deal of interaction between Parnassians and Symbolists, and it was not always clear to which group a poet belonged. In the question of free verse versus more conventional verse Heredia was perhaps more than most other Parnassians a moderator. Although he represented the second of these verse forms, he defended it calmly and not inflexibly. His broadmindedness enabled him to appreciate approaches other than the Parnassian. He listened to new points of view, showed interest in the efforts of the Symbolists, and recognized the talent of some of them. They, in turn, found qualities to admire in his poetry. It is perhaps significant that he even published a few sonnets in *La Revue blanche*, which was really a Symbolist journal. The truth is that he was so popular among the younger poets that many of them submitted their work to him simply because they felt he was genuinely interested in what they were doing.

V *The Creative Years*

Heredia did almost all his writing in the three decades following his participation in the Conférence La Bruyère. He worked slowly and steadily and his output was relatively small. Apart from one book, *Les Trophées*, in which he collected almost all of his poetry, he wrote little that was of lasting significance. His financial independence helped relieve him of pressures to meet deadlines. In spite of his painstaking manner of working, he was not a martyr in the cause of art. The image of the artist striving for perfection at the expense of great spiritual agony is not associated with Heredia; he loved life too much to devote a disproportionate number of his waking hours to writing.

But his attitude toward his art was aristocratic nonetheless. He was opposed to easy, popular art and his desire to create beauty above all is a partial explanation of the lack of abundance in his writing. A further consideration is that his poetry required a great deal of documentation and erudition. In a letter of February 2, 1872, to Georges Lafenestre, Heredia provides both of these explanations:

J'aime et je comprends trop bien le beau et je juge aussi trop justement ce que je fais, pour produire avec abondance. . . . L'art est une chose terrible aujourd'hui, car il faut tout savoir.[18]

I love and I understand beauty too well and I also judge what I do too correctly to produce abundantly. . . . Art is a terrible thing today, for it is necessary to know everything.

Heredia published many of his poems, which were mostly sonnets, on a fairly regular basis in some of the journals of the day. After the bulletin of the Conférence La Bruyère, he chose especially the *Revue française*, the *Revue de Paris* and Arsène Houssaye's *L'Artiste* during the 1860's. In the next decade he contributed to a few journals as well, but twenty-six of his sonnets appeared in the last two issues of the *Parnasse contemporain*, the first one in 1866 having contained five sonnets. During the 1880's the *Revue des deux mondes* became the journal which published most of his work. It continued to do so until after his death, when nine of his poems appeared in it posthumously in 1905. All in all thirty-nine of his poems had made their first appearance in it. In the meantime, in 1893, he had brought out *Les Trophées* with 118 sonnets, most of which had appeared previously in other publications.

After *Les Trophées* he published almost nothing. On several occasions he did compose poetry for special events. To commemorate the visit of Czar Nicholas II of Russia for the cornerstone laying of the Pont Alexandre on October 7, 1896, he wrote "Salut à l'empereur," and for the Czarina he wrote a madrigal of six stanzas. In 1903 he composed three sonnets in Spanish for the centenary of his cousin, the Cuban poet who had the same name as he. But most of his poetry that was unfinished in 1893 remained uncompleted. During the last ten or fifteen years of his life he had accepted a number of positions and responsibilities which made demands on his time and left him less time for writing. As a member of the Academy he served on the dictionary committee, represented the Academy at Leconte de Lisle's funeral, gave addresses at the unveiling or inauguration of the monuments of Du Bellay, Leconte de Lisle and Maupassant, and received Vogüé in the Academy. In 1895 he became literary director of *Le Journal*, a periodical founded by Fernand Xau, and in 1901 he accepted a position as correspondent for the paper *El Pais* of Buenos Aires. His position at the Arsenal also continued to occupy some of his time.

VI *The Last Years*

Although Heredia was fairly robust throughout most of his life, his vigor was not comparable to the volcanic energy of a Victor Hugo. Before he was fifty Heredia's health gradually began to deteriorate. For several years he was afflicted with eye problems and at times experienced double vision. Later his hearing began to fail. He often sought solitude instead of social contact and spent more time walking and meditating near his country home at Montfort l'Amaury. His hair and beard were now almost white. Near the end of his life a stomach illness added to his discomfort and he had to observe a diet whose chief component was milk. He grew less talkative, more sensitive to cold, and more inclined to indulge in reverie, especially about the past.

Heredia spent the last few months of his life in the Château de Bourdonné at Condé-sur-Vesgres. The setting of the old chateau was idyllic, and it was somehow fitting that the poet who had begun his life under a dazzling tropical sun should have had these gentle surroundings to comfort him in his last moments. He faced the prospect of death with a kind of noble serenity mingled with melancholy. In a sense, much of what he had written had to do with the inevitability of death but also with the beauty of life. On July 14, 1905, a little more than two months before his death, he wrote what was to be his last letter to his daughter Madame Henri de Régnier, telling her how much he was enjoying the beauty of life. Near the end of the letter he recalls his youth and expresses his regret at the shortness of life and beauty: "Que c'est loin, et que la vie est malheureusement courte pour un poète lyrique qui aime la beauté des choses."[19] [How long ago this was, and how short life is, unfortunately, for a lyric poet who loves the beauty of things!] He did not fear death and is reported to have said: "J'envisage la mort avec une sérénité parfaite. Mourir n'est rien. Mais vivre . . . Ah! la vie, c'est admirable!"[20] [I envisage death with perfect serenity. To die is nothing. But to live . . . Ah! Life is admirable.]

He breathed his last on October 2, 1905. His remains were taken to the Arsenal where the funeral ceremony was held on October 6, with Eugène-Melchior de Vogüé paying tribute to him on behalf of the Academy. There were many other eulogies, all stressing his goodness and his love of beauty. The next day his remains were taken to Rouen and interred in the cemetery of Notre-Dame-de-Bon-Secours, next to his mother who had died in 1877. Maurice Barrès in his *Journal officiel* of January 19, 1907, paid him this tribute:

Il dort auprès de celle qui l'avait préparé pour nous aimer. . . . Le fils des conquistadors repose sous le ciel où le vent dispersa les cendres de Jeanne d'Arc. Sa tombe accroît encore la spiritualité de ce Rouen où l'auteur du Cid enseigna l'art des vers à Jacqueline Pascal.[21]

He is sleeping near the one who had prepared him to love us. . . . The son of the conquistadores is resting under the sky where the wind scattered the ashes of Joan of Arc. His tomb adds still more to the spirituality of that Rouen where the author of the *Cid* taught the art of verse to Jacqueline Pascal.

Beside his tomb a willow can be seen trembling in the wind of the Seine and on the stone is engraved this verse of André Chénier, which Heredia especially loved: "Mon âme vagabonde à travers le feuillage/Frémira . . ." [My wandering soul will tremble through the foliage . . .] Perhaps this choice was particularly suitable, because in his last months Heredia was occupied in preparing an edition of Chénier's *Bucoliques*. An eminently fitting epitaph might have been the verses which Heredia quoted in 1894 in his address at the unveiling of Du Bellay's statue. They are Du Bellay's own:

De mourir ne suis en esmoy
Selon la loi du sort humain,
Car la meilleure part de moy
Ne craint point la fatale main.
Craigne la mort, la fortune et l'envie
A qui les Dieux n'ont donné qu'une vie.

To die I am not dismayed according to the law of human fate, for the best part of me fears not that fatal hand. Let him fear death, fate, and envy to whom the gods have given but one life.

CHAPTER 4

Trophies of Man

I *The Publication of* Les Trophées

HEREDIA'S imaginative work (as opposed to translations, discourses and critical work) consisted entirely of verse, and, as we have seen, this was by no means abundant. Apart from three Andalusian songs, a few poems of circumstance celebrating such notable people as the Russian Czar and Czarina, his "Romancero" and his "Conquérants de l'or," he wrote almost exclusively sonnets. Altogether some 140 of these were published at one time or another, eight of them posthumously. According to Armand Godoy, Heredia left behind in manuscript form about 147 more sonnets, largely in fragment form.[1] Of the completed sonnets, he selected only 118 to figure in his collected poetry appearing on February 16, 1893, under the title *Les Trophées*. He is thus essentially an author known for a single book.

The oldest poems in *Les Trophées* had first been published in 1863. More than two dozen had not been published before. The collection thus represents the work of about thirty years, a long period of time indeed for such a slim volume. And yet until late in Heredia's life it was by no means certain that he would even publish a collection of his verse.

On the other hand, it appears likely that he had given some thought much earlier to the possibility of collecting his sonnets according to some unifying principle. In the opinion of Xavier de Ricard he had conceived such an idea as early as 1866.[2] At that time he had published five sonnets in the first *Parnasse contemporain*. One of these, "Fleurs de feu," was to have been the title of the collection. Perhaps this had been suggested by Baudelaire's *Fleurs du mal*, by then already in its second edition. In any case, nothing came of his plans, if he really had any serious ones at that time. Perhaps *Fleurs de feu* proved to be too limiting in scope for his conception of the whole.

In the third *Parnasse contemporain*, 1876, he published twenty-five sonnets, the largest group before *Les Trophées*. Was this a kind of preliminary sample of his 1893 collection? Ibrovac believes it was.[3] All these sonnets reappeared in *Les Trophées* and nearly in the same relative order. Although sub-titles are not given in the *Parnasse contemporain*, the subject matter represents all the groups found in the final collection: Greece with nine sonnets, Rome with one, the Renaissance with seven, the Orient with one, and Nature and Dream with seven.

While the idea of publishing his sonnets in some kind of organized whole seemed to appeal to Heredia, he continued to hesitate. He was in the unusual position of enjoying almost immediate literary esteem and admiration without so far having published a book. His poems were admired, copied out, pasted in albums, learned by heart and recited in literary circles. In any event, Heredia was not much concerned about literary fame and his livelihood did not depend on receipts from book sales. He did not need to hurry on that account.

The delay probably had more to do with other factors. He was a perfectionist for whom it was a point of honor not to offer the public anything but his best work. The painstaking slowness that characterized the composition of his sonnets was reflected in the process of organizing the whole. He seemed to have difficulty with the problem of arranging the poems and could not obtain the "noble ordonnance" (noble order) which he sought.[4] In addition he was afraid the collection might not be sufficiently complete. Perhaps he was aware of gaps in the groupings he envisaged. As late as 1891, when Pierre Louÿs asked him why he did not publish his poems as a collection, Heredia replied: "Parce qu'ils ne sont pas achevés. *Les Trophées*, ce sont mes sonnets. Quand j'aurai un volume de sonnets je le publierai. Aujourd'hui ce ne serait qu'une plaquette."[5] [Because they are not completed. *Les Trophées* are my sonnets. . . . When I have a volume of sonnets, I shall publish it. Today it would only be a booklet.]

It is thus clear that by this time he had at least chosen a title. In 1892 he withdrew to the solitude of the country, where he examined all his poems once more. It must have been on this occasion that he finally decided to publish them and that he made his final selection and grouping. Perhaps he felt about the collection as Valéry felt about a poem: that it can never actually be finished, only abandoned. At whatever point Heredia decided to publish it, no matter how long he were to wait, the collection would not really be complete or perfect.

The success of the volume was never in doubt. The nearly 5,000 copies put out by Alphonse Lemerre in the first printing were sold out at ten francs a copy in a matter not of days or weeks but of hours. To the sonnets he had selected, Heredia had decided at the last moment to add his "Romancero" consisting of three poems, and his "Conquérants de l'or." The book was discussed everywhere and met with widespread admiration. Painters and engravers came forward to offer their services to illustrate it. In one month newspapers and journals published more than a hundred articles on *Les Trophées* and reproduced most of the poems in the book. The French Academy awarded him the 6,000 franc prize of the "Concours Archon-Despérouses." Such success was all the more remarkable because it came at the height of the Symbolist period. Symbolist reviews, which normally tended to be critical of Parnassian poetry, were generous in recognizing Heredia's talent. A writer could hardly have imagined a better public reaction.

II *Poems of Greece and Sicily*

The subject matter of *Les Trophées* may be said to encompass all of human time. The first group of sonnets, thirty-nine in all, is the largest and appears under the heading "La Grèce et la Sicile." The poems in this group give us a view of life from its beginnings. The world they present is old in the sense that it is far removed from us in time, but young because it is situated at the beginning of time. It is inhabited by nymphs, satyrs, centaurs, gods and mythological heroes. Perseus and Andromeda, Jason and Medea, Bacchus and Ariadne, Apollo, Adonis, Artemis, Aphrodite, Pan and Hercules are among the principal actors on its stage. Gradually, as time passes, they give way to human beings. The high gods are less frequently presented than the lesser divinities, whose destiny is closer to that of man, and it is after all the condition of man that interests Heredia most.

It is not difficult to find in the Greek poems a sense of historical progression in the evocation of selected moments from Greek life. "La Naissance d'Aphrodite" is a key poem in this connection because it presents some notion of Greek cosmology as interpreted by Heredia. It takes us to pre-history, when Chaos enveloped all, when space and time were undifferentiated, when the splendors of spring sunlight and the plenty of summer's harvests were still unknown. Few details of cosmic creation are provided. However, at the time of Aphrodite's birth the gods of snowy Olympus were uncultured and ignorant of laughter and play. A fertile rain from heaven caused the ocean to open, allowing Aphrodite to emerge in her radiant, naked beauty, like a flower out of the ocean foam, which was red with the blood of Uranus.

In this sonnet we notice an indication of two themes which recur in a significantly large number of Greek sonnets. Both of them find their logical place in a historical sequence whose point of departure is the creation of the world. One of them is the freshness and purity of the newly-created world. The other is a certain primitive and even violent aspect of early life. "La Naissance d'Aphrodite" suggests this freshness and purity through its reference to the beauties of spring and summer and the radiance of Aphrodite; the violence is embodied by the gods of Olympus.

The dominant impression contained in many of Heredia's poems of early Greece is that the world is new, unspoiled and fresh. This is true especially of the natural world. Forests are calm and green and allow the sun's rays to filter through their leaves to create enchanting patterns of light and shadow. Vegetation is rich, skies are azure, and lakes are silvery. Another common element in these early landscapes is the crystalline brooks. The air has about it a certain magic, as if to express earliest man's childlike sense of wonder at the miracle of the creation of the world and of life itself. Its purity is matched by the white and fresh beauty of the naked bodies of the nymphs or by the warm moonlight flooding the scene of the nocturnal dance to the rhythms of Pan's pipes.

But this paradisiacal existence, even from the beginning, seems precarious and short-lived. Desire, passion, violence, and a certain primitive savagery are the forces which threaten it and in fact end it. In "La Chasse," for example, we read:

> Le Soleil, à travers les cimes incertaines
> Et l'ombre où rit le timbre argentin des fontaines,
> Se glisse, darde et luit en jeux étincelants.

The sun, through the indistinct treetops and the shadows where the fountain laughs with silvery voice, filters in, darts and shines in sparkling playfulness.

This sonnet is but one of several in which the sylvan calm is broken by the sudden intrusion of Artemis, goddess of the hunt, hair streaming in the wind, full of fierce energy, invincible, bringing terror to the woods and its inhabitants, and herself experiencing what appears to be a certain masochistic pleasure in mingling her blood with that of the slaughtered victims. Animals cannot escape from Artemis and men are not safe from animals. The Nemean lion strikes terror in the hearts of the inhabitants of the valley of Nemea. In "Némée" the herdsman turns around wide-eyed with fear as he sees the lion suddenly emerge at the edge of the forest. An epic struggle then ensues between the beast and Hercules. The sun disappears and the sky is blood-red as if to testify to the superhuman dimension of the struggle. The victor is of course Hercules, who is called "un monstrueux héros" (a monstrous hero). In a sense he represents, probably more than any other single individual in the Greek poems, the primitive violence of early times. He is monstrous because in him are mingled human and animal elements. The physical struggle between him and the lion literally unites man and beast, and the lion's skin which he wears further symbolizes this. Indeed Heredia appears to forget his divine ancestry, calling him a man.

Hercules can also be called heroic because some of his exploits have the effect of liberating men from natural dangers that threaten them. Thus, after presenting the destruction of the monster of Nemea, Heredia in "Stymphale" evokes Hercules' battle with the legendary Stymphalian birds, which ate human flesh. As he releases his arrows, the slain birds fall like a "pluie horrible" (horrible rain). Other violent acts of Hercules involve the centaurs, who are invited to a marriage feast given by their former enemies, the Lapithae. In "Centaures et Lapithes" one of the centaurs tries to defile the bride. Hercules intervenes and in "Fuite des Centaures" gives chase to the fleeing centaurs, who are drunk with murder and rebellion, but nonetheless filled with fear of their formidable pursuer.

Other examples of violence could be cited. The jealous fury of Medea ("Jason et Medée") and the devastating punishment inflicted on Andromeda ("Andromède au monstre"), chained to a rock as a sacrifice to a sea-monster, are two such incidents that come to mind. Another sonnet, "Le Thermodon," recalls the defeat of the Amazons. Perhaps this is the bloodiest of all Heredia's Greek sonnets. To the extent that it represents the effects of mass murder and war at any time or place, it is not specifically Greek. The war itself is evoked only in the first two verses:

> Vers Thémiscyre en feu qui tout le jour trembla
> Des clameurs et du choc de la cavalerie . . .

In the direction of Themiscyra on fire which shook all day from the clamor
and the clash of the cavalry . . .

It is rather the effect, the tragic silence after the battle, which im-
presses Heredia. The stream is filled with bodies, weapons and
blood. Its shores are strewn with dead Amazon virgins, likened to
giant lilies felled by a harvester's scythe. The only sign of life is
provided by the fleeing stallions, once white, but now red with
Amazon blood.

Animal desire and sensual passion are also linked with primitive
life in the Greek poems. It is probably no coincidence that we find in
them so many figures who are part animal and part human or divine,
such creatures as, in addition to the centaurs, Pan and the Sphinx. By
their dual nature they point to the struggle between, or at least co-
existence of, animal instincts and man's higher aspirations, rational
and creative. These beings, however, are dominated largely by their
baser feelings. The lascivious Pan, his eyes burning with desire, lurks
in hiding, seeking an opportunity to surprise and carry off an unsuspecting naked nymph into the dense forest, accompanying this
act with mocking laughter ("Pan"). In "Le Bain des nymphes" he is
compared to a sinister crow frightening the swans. But Pan lacks insight into his nature and is not troubled by it.

In some of the centaurs we find an awakening of a sense of
awareness. "La Centauresse" and "Nessus" complement each other,
the first emphasizing animal heat and the second human desire. In
both sonnets we notice that the world which is evoked is no longer a
freshly-created one in which there is no sense of a past. On the contrary, both the centauress and Nessus are keenly aware of the past,
when life seemed much better. Nostalgia was not possible before.
Now both recall a former state corresponding to their idea of original
happiness. Both have a vague sense of a kind of paradise lost. Nessus
especially links this past happiness to a state of innocence, when he
was blissfully ignorant of a different fate. But, as in the drama of
Eden, he has tasted the fruit of the tree of knowledge in the form of
his awakening of carnal desire for Hercules' wife Deianira:

> Mais depuis que j'ai vu l'Epouse triomphale
> Sourire entre les bras de l'Archer de Stymphale,
> Le désir me harcèle et hérisse mes crins:

But ever since I saw the triumphant spouse smiling in the arms of the archer
of Stymphalus desire tortures me and makes my hair stand on end.

The happiness of the centauress, on the other hand, ended when the centaurs abandoned her and the other centauresses in search of human mates. She now becomes aware of the distant call of stallions and realizes that her awakening desire for an animal constitutes for her and her comrades a degradation, a fall:

> C'ėst que leur amour même aux brutes nous ravale;
> Le cri qu'il nous arrache est un hennissement,
> Et leur désir en nous n'étreint que la cavale.

It is because their love brings us right down to the animal level. The cry which it draws from us is a neighing, and their desire embraces only the mare in us.

It is tempting to see in the centaurs' preference for human mates a symbolic expression of a point in man's evolution when he senses the possibility of a more elevated life. But the other side of the coin shows that he cannot free himself from some of the lower instincts which stand in the way of his noblest aspirations. Nessus regards his newly-found human desire as a curse of the gods:

> Car un Dieu, maudit soit le nom dont il se nomme!
> A mêlé dans le sang enfiévré de mes reins
> Au rut de l'étalon l'amour qui dompte l'homme.

For a God, cursed be his name, has mingled in the feverish blood of my loins the heat of the stallion with the love which enslaves man.

The victim of the sorceress in "La Magicienne" also blames the gods for his plight. His dilemma is that on the one hand he finds her charms overpowering; the gods have given her kisses, tears and intoxicating lips as weapons which make her irresistible. On the other hand, he finds these dark enchantments and sinister charms odious. Unlike the centaurs, he feels a sense of guilt and regards his enslavement to his sensual instincts as a divine punishment.

"Sphinx" presents yet another aspect of this problem, namely the destructiveness of desire. The Sphinx, "La vierge aux ailes d'aigle" (the virgin with the wings of an eagle), is "the one who strangles," the she-monster which in Greek mythology is said to have killed those Thebans who were unable to answer the riddle she proposed to them. Heredia, however, makes of her a creature resembling Leconte de Lisle's Ekhidna, another she-monster, infinitely

desirable, but killing those whom she embraces. A dialogue between
the lover and Heredia's Sphinx ends as follows:

> . . . — Qu'importe le supplice,
> Si j'ai conquis la gloire et ravi le baiser?
> — Tu triomphes en vain, car tu meurs. — O délice!

What does the torture matter if I have conquered glory and stolen the kiss?
— You triumph in vain for you will die. — O delight!

The sonnet amply underscores the dual aspect of love. From the
standpoint of the lover it brings both pleasure and suffering.
However, the intensity of the experience is such that he seems willing to suffer for it. Symbolically through its embodiment in the
Sphinx it is both beautiful and monstrous, or at least so it appears.
Recalling the enigmatic aspects of the mythological Sphinx, Heredia
may in fact be pointing to the possibility that it is illusory.

Illusion or reality, it is nonetheless part of man's condition.
Irresistible desire, primitive violence, the destructive forces of nature
— all these beset man and separate him from his paradisiacal beginnings. But these are still not the most sobering aspects of his existence. However imperfect his life may be, he clings to it realizing
that it is brief and that death is final. Heredia's Greek poems express
no hope of a better fate. Living beings, from the humble
grasshopper mourned by the little child whose tender tears wash the
tiny tomb it has erected ("Epigramme funéraire") to the lesser
divinities themselves, are all mortal.

How do these mortals imagine death and what aspects of it does
Heredia choose to present? Physically little remains. In "Marsyas"
the satyr's bones are dissolved and his blood mingled with the mountain streams. Only his skin is left, a tattered remnant attached to the
trunk of a yew tree. It flutters in the wind which plays with it at will.
His flute has been silenced forever by Apollo's cruel act of torture. In
"Le Naufragé" the shipwrecked mariner's bones have been washed
up on some desolate shore and covered with sand by the wind.
Perhaps nowhere else does Heredia express so absolutely the finality
of death:

> Au pli le plus profond de la mouvante dune,
> En la nuit sans aurore et sans astre et sans lune,
> Que le navigateur trouve enfin le repos.

In the deepest fold of the moving dune, in the night without sunrise and
without stars and moon, may the navigator finally find rest.

In "La Prière du mort" a young man whose message comes from the
realm of the dead envisages his flesh as devoured by wolves, and he
pictures his white-haired mother mourning over his tomb, a vain
tomb, he says, because it is empty. The young bride in "La Jeune
Morte" evokes in accents reminiscent of André Chénier her vision of
death. Both the joy of living and the tragedy of death gain intensity
from their confrontation on the happy occasion of her marriage:

> Mes yeux sont fermés à la lumière heureuse,
> Et maintenant j'habite, hélas! et pour jamais,
> L'inexorable Erèbe et la Nuit Ténébreuse.

My eyes have closed to the happy light and now, alas, I inhabit, and forever,
inexorable Erebus and somber night.

Despite the physical disintegration of the dead their final destination or state is Erebus, a word signifying darkness. What remains of
the dead is almost always called "ombre" (shade) in these Greek
poems. It may be recalled that Erebus himself in Classical
mythology was the son of Chaos, who enveloped all things before
creation and so represents the pre-created state. The descent of the
"shades" of the dead to join the darkness of Erebus thus suggests a
return to the darkness from which they sprang and in which they are
now destined to remain forever.

To this point we have been considering mostly negative aspects of
the human condition as seen to a large extent through Greek
mythology. But the lost purity of the newly-created world, the
menacing forces of nature, man's primitive and sensual instincts,
and finally his mortal nature, do not form a complete picture of his
existence. Such an image does not take into account his nobler
aspirations, his dreams and his efforts to improve his condition.
In this connection let us consider the sonnet "L'Esclave," included in the subsection "Epigrammes et Bucoliques" of the Greek
poems:

> Tel, nu, sordide, affreux, nourri des plus vils mets,
> Esclave — vois, mon corps en a gardé les signes —
> Je suis né libre au fond du golfe aux belles lignes
> Où l'Hybla plein de miel mire ses bleus sommets.

J'ai quitté l'île heureuse, hélas! . . . Ah! si jamais
Vers Syracuse et les abeilles et les vignes
Tu retournes, suivant le vol vernal des cygnes,
Cher hôte, informe-toi de celle que j'aimais.

Reverrai-je ses yeux de sombre violette,
Si purs, sourire au ciel natal qui s'y reflète
Sous l'arc victorieux que tend un sourcil noir?

Sois pitoyable! Pars, va, cherche Cléariste
Et dis-lui que je vis encor pour la revoir.
Tu la reconnaîtras, car elle est toujours triste.

Thus, naked, sordid, frightful, nourished with vilest food, a slave — see, my
body still shows signs of it — I was born free at the end of the gulf with its
beautiful contours, where Hybla full of honey mirrors its blue summits. I left
the happy isle, alas! . . . Ah, if ever toward Syracuse and the bees and the
vineyards you should return, following the vernal flight of the swans, dear
companion, inquire about the one I loved. Shall I see again her eyes of dark
violet, so pure, smiling under the native sky they reflect beneath the victorious arch of a dark eyebrow? Have pity! Leave, go, look for Clearista and
tell her that I still live to see her again. You will recognize her, for she is
always sad.

This sonnet alerts us to the passage of time. It makes us think of a
more recent age in Greek history than that of Hercules and the centaurs. We notice some striking changes. The slave is a fallen man, in
a sense; he has lost his freedom and has been separated from his
home and his loved one. But he is no longer a primitive being; he is a
man of dreams, filled with nostalgia for the Eden he has lost. His
love is as delicate and pure as the Eve of whom he dreams. His voice
speaks for all those who hear in the depths of their souls echoes of the
far-away music of paradise.

Situated between distant Eden and the prospect of certain and
final death, men are all slaves, and their attempts to achieve liberation consist in trying to restore at least some aspects of Eden, or in
looking for ways to cheat the finality of death. At least, that is the
way in which men and even some mythological figures react in
Heredia's Greek poems. We have already seen how Hercules com-
batted certain forces of nature such as the Nemean lion and the
Stymphalian birds. Symbolically the struggle of Hercules, a solar
deity, against the centaurs, descendants of clouds, could be envisaged as the struggle for enlightenment and purification against

the forces of obscurity. But even the centaurs are not totally benighted, since they are aware of their enslavement to animal passions. The group of three sonnets, "Andromède au monstre," "Persée et Andromède" and "Le Ravissement d'Andromède," serves as an outstanding example of liberation and elevation. In these three sonnets Perseus on the fabled, winged Pegasus comes to rescue Andromeda, chained to an ocean rock, and then carries her off. Their flight is cosmic, taking them far above the earth until they glimpse whole continents (in a manner reminiscent of the experiences of our modern astronauts). They rise higher and higher into the blue of the night and ethereal stellar space, flying from star to star. We find no suggestion here of animal instincts. Andromeda is "la vierge aux cheveux d'or" (the golden-haired virgin). The whole drama of the rescue and the physical flight symbolizes the release from an earthbound existence and the ascent to a spiritual domain.

We must concede, of course, that the accomplishments of mythological heroes are by definition superhuman. But we notice also the beginnings of a tendency among ordinary mortals to translate their higher aspirations into heroic action and superior accomplishments. "Le Naufragé," for example, presents the mariner happy and proud to pit his courage and strength against the dangers of the sea, thereby risking his life. In "Epigramme votive" the aging warrior contemplates what is left of the weapons with which he distinguished himself on the field of battle. "Le Coureur" and "Le Cocher" pay tribute to athletic accomplishments. The first of these evokes the almost superhuman efforts of Alexander the Great's runner Ladas straining every muscle and fibre of his being in his boundless drive to extend himself as he strives constantly toward difficult goals. The second glorifies the skill and daring of the famous Lybian charioteer Porphyrus, who has surpassed even the divine Castor, celebrated for his mastery of horses.

While high aspirations and heroic action represent the dominant manner in which men and gods react to life in Heredia's Greek poems, we notice another attitude as well. We find this in a smaller number of poems mostly devoted to simple people in a pastoral setting. This attitude is characterized by a tranquil acceptance of life, often but not always with joy. Perhaps it is best represented by the herdsmen, who are almost always at peace with the world and their own lot, and feel in harmony with life. As long as they make the required sacrifices to Pan, god of the flocks and herds, they can enjoy the simple pleasures of life. Some of these herdsmen can be found in the two sonnets "Le Chevrier" and "Les Bergers." In these two poems Pan appears not in the least villainous. In the first he makes the goats dance to the music of his pipes in the moonlight, thus adding to the pleasure of the herdsman, who with a companion is enjoying a simple fare of figs and wine. In "Les Bergers" the shepherds are confident that Pan is well disposed toward the simple sacrifice made to him. The speaker has no material cares; his animals will provide cheese and milk and the nymphs will weave a mantle of wool. Meanwhile he can experience the pleasure of sleeping on the grass near a spring in the shade of a tree and listen to the music of its leaves.

Perhaps the best example of complete acceptance is found in "Le Laboureur." This sonnet concerns an aged plowman, who has spent all his life on the land:

> Près d'un siècle, au soleil, sans en être plus riche,
> Il a poussé le coutre au travers de la friche;
> Ayant vécu sans joie, il vieillit sans remords.

For nearly a century, in the sun, without getting richer from it, he has pushed the colter through the fallow. Having lived without joy, he grows old without regret.

He knows no other life, he has never questioned anything, and he has never attempted to change anything. But now he is too old for these labors. He realizes that death is near and, simple as he is, he is incapable of picturing it as anything other than a continuation of his present life. He thinks he will have to keep on plowing in the shady fields watered by Erebus.

Although the plowman is not sophisticated, his attitude toward death is not so different from that which we find generally in the Greek poems. It is true that for him it means only a change of location; otherwise his life's activities will continue as before. But the essential point is that he cannot conceive that death can be final, irreversible and inexorable. And in this respect he is by no means alone. Although others speak of the finality of death, their concept of it is only intellectual; they cannot really envisage total annihilation. As we saw earlier, their shade ("ombre") remains — and whatever else "ombre" may signify, it is not nothingness, since some manifestation of consciousness or sensation is usually attached to it.

The young bride in "La Jeune Morte," for example, stricken on the eve of her marriage, still "hears" the creeping vines and ants. In "Regilla" the shade of the dead Regilla still counts the days and months since she last saw her lover, hoping he will come to her. The refusal or inability to accept the finality of death as complete annihilation is manifested also in the prospect of resurrection and in the attempt to achieve permanence through some enduring monument. The theme of resurrection is rare in the Greek sonnets, but it occurs, for example, in "Le Reveil d'un dieu," which presents the myth of Adonis, in which an unusually generous gesture of the gods permits Adonis to come back to the earth each year to spend six months with Astarte. The destiny of Perseus and Andromeda is somewhat unusual too: as their flight takes them heavenward through starry space they see their constellation being born as an eternal monument to their existence.

These considerations also throw further light on the heroic accomplishments which we have already noticed. These are motivated not only by man's desire to liberate his higher self but also, I think, by his wish to be immortal. In a sense his achievements can be considered as monuments. If we recall "Le Cocher," for example, we find that the chariot driver, after leaving all his rivals far behind, undergoes a kind of apotheosis. The sight of his fiery chariot, Heredia suggests, may be too much for mortal eyes.

Still another way mankind seeks immortality is through concrete objects, more durable than human flesh, and especially through art objects. We may take "Epigramme votive" as an illustration. Here the aging warrior, no longer strong enough to bend the bow which at one time he alone was able to bend, asks that all his weapons be hung up. Only his arrows are missing but they can be found on the field of Marathon, a testimonial to his accomplishments. In the category of art objects two sonnets come to mind. One of these is "Le Coureur," which really evokes a statue of the runner, rather than the runner himself. But it is precisely the statue which attempts to make him immortal. For those who contemplate it, Ladas is still real, alive, and running as he used to run. His muscles are tensed, perspiration beads his brow and he gasps for breath as he strains to reach the finish line. The other sonnet is "Le Vase." This one differs from the preceding examples in that its meaning is more general. Instead of seeking to immortalize any one individual, the chiseled ivory of the vase records impressions of a number of moments and figures from Greek mythology and history, including Jason, Medea, the golden fleece, the Nile, the Bacchantes, a battle scene, and the Chimeras.

We may well ask at this point to what degree man in the Greek ᷉oems has succeeded in his aspirations and efforts. The very first of ᷉ese poems, "L'Oubli," I think, supplies an answer:

> Le temple est en ruine au haut du promontoire.
> Et la Mort a mêlé, dans ce fauve terrain,
> Les Déesses de marbre et les Héros d'airain
> Dont l'herbe solitaire ensevelit la gloire.
>
> Seul, parfois, un bouvier menant ses buffles boire,
> De sa conque où soupire un antique refrain
> Emplissant le ciel calme et l'horizon marin,
> Sur l'azur infini dresse sa forme noire.
>
> La Terre maternelle et douce aux anciens Dieux
> Fait à chaque printemps, vainement éloquente,
> Au chapiteau brisé verdir une autre acanthe;
>
> Mais l'Homme indifférent au rêve des aïeux
> Ecoute sans frémir, du fond des nuit sereines,
> La Mer qui se lamente en pleurant les Sirènes.

The temple is in ruins high on the promontory, and death has intermingled in this wild terrain marble goddesses and heroes of bronze, whose glory lies buried under the solitary grass. Alone, at times, a herdsman, taking his cattle to drink, filling the calm sky and the marine horizon with his shell in which sighs an ancient refrain, stands with his dark form against the endless azure. Mother earth, gentle to the ancient gods, each springtime makes another acanthus green, vainly eloquent on the broken capital. But man, indifferent to the dreams of his ancestors, listens without trembling to the sea which, from out of the depths of the serene nights, laments, weeping for the sirens.

Perhaps the word which most completely summarizes the impressions left by this sonnet is "futility." Man's efforts do not count for much after all. Even his most durable artifacts made of marble or bronze are not lasting, and his ephemeral condition is sharply emphasized by the contrast with the immutability of nature, represented here by its larger elements, the sky, the sea and the earth. Even the lowly grass, which obliterates his last traces, is stronger than he. And yet man still preserves an "ancient refrain," testifying to the continuity of the race. Like the cycles of nature, each man begins his dream anew for himself and in his own way.

III   *Rome and the Barbarians*

The group of poems collected under the heading "Rome et les Barbares" consists of only twenty-three sonnets. They present various elements of Roman civilization, including its everyday aspect, glimpses of life in the colonies, especially on Gallic soil, suggestions of the more urbane and voluptuous life of Rome with its inherent decadence, as well as some of the military and political crises which did not figure among the most glorious hours of the Empire.

As we begin reading these sonnets it is evident almost immediately that the chronological perspective has changed from the Greek poems, but the break is not abrupt. The very first sonnet, "Pour le Vaisseau de Virgile," serves as a transition between the Greek and Roman world by introducing the Latin poet Virgil. This announces a new age, but it is also in part a spatial transition, since the sonnet is really a prayer for the safety of Virgil's voyage to the Hellenic world as he journeys "sur la mer sacrée où chantait Arion, / Vers la terre des Dieux . . . " (on the sacred sea where Arion sang toward the land of the gods . . .). This is the last we shall hear in this section of the enchanted shores of Greece. Apart from a sonnet or two recalling the pastoral flavor of the "Epigrammes et Bucoliques" in the Greek section, the tone of the Roman poems is different. Perhaps their most striking aspect is a feeling of distance, of progression in time. Gone is the freshness of the world at its beginnings when deities and humans inhabited a new earth together and were alive to its enchantment. But gone also is the primitivism of that world. The savagery of some of that primitivism gives way in the Roman sonnets to the more systematic violence of war, while the sense of wonder and freshness of outlook are replaced by urbane sophistication or nostalgic longing for a simpler life and for the days when communication with the gods was a reality.

Perhaps the central fact about Rome as presented by Heredia is the weakening or loss of its sense of the divine and its arrogant reliance on its own strength. The divine is conspicuously absent in those poems connected with life in Rome, with the exception of the five sonnets grouped under the heading "Hortorum Deus." These five are devoted to the rural gods of Rome, notably Priapus, god of fruitfulness, protector of vines and gardens, who sees to it that

strangers and children do not intrude. In some ways his lot is not unpleasant: the seasons adorn him with their special charms; his important responsibilities and status give him a certain satisfaction; the
proprietor whose property he protects is honest, virtuous and ap-
preciative; and twice a year a young buck is sacrificed on his rustic
altar. All in all his existence, though not illustrious, has a certain un-
spectacular wholesomeness. Yet he complains that the life of a rural
god can be hard, and he envies the easier life of some other
household gods, who are more sheltered from the elements and more
involved with the personal lives of the families which house them.
But his real tragedy is that he is a fallen god. Formerly, he recalls, his
form rose proudly above the prow of a galley as it faced the prospect
and excitement of marine adventure. His glory has vanished. Instead
of being in a position of leadership, he is now a servant, and a lowly
one at that.

Perhaps his fate parallels that of Rome, also about to fall from
greatness. There is little sense of the divine in those sonnets evoking
the life of the capital and the more sophisticated and decadent
elements of Roman civilization. In this connection we think of the
sonnets devoted to Rome's wars, but there are others as well. In
"Tranquillus" we can find suggestions of imperial vice. The poem
conveys some aspects of the life of the writer Suetonius, who retires
to the country every autumn not only because he wants to get away
from the agitation of urban Rome to a calm pastoral existence but
also, it appears, to escape from the emperors such as Nero, Claudius
and Caligula, who haunt him even in his retreat. Here he fights back
by writing in a sharp satirical style about the "noirs loisirs du
vieillard de Caprée" (the dark leisure activities of the old man of
Capri), a reference to the debauchery of Tiberius.

The sonnet "Lupercus," which imitates the style of Martial,
attempts to provide some flavor of Rome's literary world and
specifically to reproduce an example of its sophisticated wit. Written
mostly in dialogue, it brings together Lupercus and the epigram-
matist Martial, whose latest work has just appeared. Lupercus, not
wishing to spend money, asks whether he may send his servant to
borrow Martial's complete works. The poet replies that Lupercus'
servant is old and feeble, that it would be too far to go, and that in
any case, since the bookseller lives close to Lupercus, the latter can
find Martial's works for sale beside those of Virgil, Silius, Pliny,
Terence and Phaedrus. Not only has he squelched Lupercus, but he
has also ranked himself among the best Roman writers.

"Le Tepidarium" suggests another component of Roman life, the quest for luxury and sensual pleasure. It presents a remarkably well integrated pattern of impressions appealing to most of our senses and heavy with exotic and voluptuous suggestion focusing on an Asian beauty. It is difficult to imagine a more sensuous evocation. In this sonnet alone Heredia has succeeded in compressing the exotic and perhaps, for Rome, the decadent and debilitating aspects of the eastern part of its empire.

Sensuous beauty is found also in a trilogy of sonnets grouped under the general heading "Antoine et Cléopâtre." The dark and exotic charm of Cleopatra is unmistakably linked with the personal destiny of Antony and with the fate of the Roman Empire as well. The atmosphere in "Le Cydnus," the first of these three sonnets, is not unlike that of "Le Tepidarium." The air is laden with heavy perfumes, the music of flutes, and the rustling of silk, while visual details also emphasize the richness of the setting. Here the enchantress Cleopatra appears in the splendor of the evening at Tarsus, where she is to meet Antony, who has fallen under the spell of her charms. Like a bird of prey observing her victim from a distance, she also reminds us of the fatal Romantic heroine type, destroyer and destroyed, but unaware that desire is linked with its somber companion death.

The second sonnet of the trilogy, "Soir de Bataille," evokes the carnage of a bloody battle in Asia Minor. Roman soldiers fall like autumn leaves before the onslaught of the enemy's archers. Still Roman pride refuses to be broken. Rome's colors still fly, its fanfare still sounds, as the emperor appears against the red sky, superb and erect on his horse, in spite of the fact that he is bristling with arrows and bleeding freely. In the third sonnet, probably the best known of the three, Antony is cast in a distinctly less heroic role. Undaunted by arrows on the field of battle, he nevertheless easily becomes the captive of the voluptuous Cleopatra, locked in his embrace. Together they look out over the Nile and then, as he gazes into her eyes, the latter appear to foreshadow doom, for he sees in them "Toute une mer immense où fuyaient des galères" (An entire and immense sea on which galleys were fleeing).

Heredia has chosen to present another dark moment in the history of the Roman Empire in the two sonnets "La Trebbia" and "Après Cannes," which evoke Hannibal's victories over Rome during the Punic Wars. The first of these presents a glimpse of the camp of the Roman legions. It is morning. Many signs indicate that the Romans should not attack. Scipion's advice, the augurs, the overflowing of

the Trebbia River, the wind, the rain — all these appear to be un-
favorable omens. However, Consul Sempronius, proud and eager for
glory, ignores these ominous forebodings. Meanwhile the horizon is
red with villages set ablaze and the Carthaginian elephants can be
heard trumpeting in the distance. Hannibal, confident and already
triumphant, calmly awaits the arrival of the Roman legions.
    In "Après Cannes" the scene is Rome itself. As in "La Trebbia,"
of which it is a companion piece, we find an atmosphere of impend-
ing doom. The young men are gone to war and the city is left to the
plebeians, slaves, children, women, and old men, all of whom sense
their helplessness. Having heard of Roman defeats elsewhere, they
live in terror and anxiously look toward the Sabine mountains, expecting at any moment to see Hannibal on his elephant rising above
them.
    The disasters associated with the poems concerning Antony and
the Punic Wars could suggest to our minds the title "Sic transit
gloria." They demonstrate the futility of military might and domina-
tion over others. Even the most powerful empires must crumble and
man's pride, power and glory are transient. Similarly, as Antony
learns, physical beauty is deceptive. And the superstitions to which
the Romans increasingly cling as the might of their empire crumbles
appear empty compared to the more elevated and noble spiritual
values which we can find elsewhere in *Les Trophées*.
    Having shown the vanity of power and sensual pleasure, Heredia
makes it clear that other attitudes and other ways of reacting to the
human condition existed within the empire. One of these was the
quest for the simple life. We have already seen that in "Tranquillus"
the writer Suetonius is trying to escape from vice-ridden Rome. But
that is not the only reason for his retreat; he is also looking for a
simpler way of life in his humble villa surrounded by his vineyard.
Perhaps the best expression of the ideal of the simple life is found in
"Villula." It evokes the last years of the aging poet Gallus. He is
spending them in his little villa under a thatched roof, in the woods
on a Cisalpine slope where he was born. His wants are few:

> Il a sa vigne, un four à cuire plus d'un pain,
> Et dans son potager foisonne le lupin.
> C'est peu? Gallus n'a pas désiré davantage.

He has his vineyard, an oven to bake more than one loaf of bread, and in his
vegetable garden the lupine abound. That is little? Gallus did not wish any
more.

Gallus knows the futility of glory and that is why he is "satisfait de son destin borné" (content with his limited lot). Now we know, states the last verse of the sonnet, that Gallus is a wise man. Perhaps it is true that such aspirations indicate wisdom. The choice, at any rate, was made by men such as Gallus and Suetonius, who had an alternative, who had known a more complex urban life and had found it wanting. However, we find this need for an uncomplicated pastoral existence in others as well, in simple people who have never experienced a more sophisticated way of life. As in certain of the Greek poems, where Heredia introduces a similar theme, the herdsman more than any one else appears to represent such a manner of living. "La Flûte," for example, paints an idealized picture of the goat herd. It is evening. Among the rushes flows a cool spring, and nearby a goat and her kid are quietly grazing. The herdsman is invited to stretch out on the soft grass in the shade and to allow his sighs of love to mingle in harmonious breath with the music of the pipes. Though the scene is rustic, it is somewhat stylized and reminiscent of bucolic literary conventions.

More primitive and rooted in the earth is the rustic existence presented in a number of sonnets under the heading "Sonnets épigraphes." These are dated Bagnères-de-Luchon, September, 188 . . . The Pyrenees, which are the setting for these poems, were well known to Heredia. When he was young he visited his relatives there on more than one occasion. It was in his hotel at Bagnères-de-Luchon that he happened to come across a book by Julien Sacaze entitled *Epigraphie de Luchon.* Casual curiosity soon led to profound interest in its contents, which inspired Heredia to write this group of sonnets consisting of "Le Voeu," "La Source," "Le Dieu Hêtre," "Aux Montagnes divines" and "L'Exilée." Each of these is preceded by an epigraph or epigraphs corresponding to inscriptions found on votive altars in the region.

The attachment to the earth which we notice in most of these sonnets has a dimension which is absent in those presenting the rural retreats of eminent Romans. It has to do, not with convention, taste or logic, but with deeply rooted instincts linked with man's need to cling to something permanent. Here we feel that man in contact with nature is aware of being in the presence of supernatural forces. These poems celebrate nature and its gods. Nature is animated and we are reminded of some of the Greek sonnets, so much so that the sudden appearance of a nymph, faun or other natural deity would hardly be a surprise. Roman gods are intermingled with the older gods of the first inhabitants of the French Pyrenees. The first two epigraphic sonnets, "Le Voeu" and "La Source," both celebrate the thermal springs, stressing their eternity. The Iberians, the Gauls, the Gascons and the Romans have all in their turn experienced their beautiful effects and each race has left some altar or other tribute recognizing something divine in the springs. Even now the Romans sing their divine song and make the poet also want to erect an altar to the subterranean nymphs.

But time has weakened man's vital contact with the gods. In "La Source" the altar to the spring is overgrown with vines and grass, and the plaintive sound coming from the spring is the song of the nymph lamenting the fact that it is forgotten. The waters are an "inutile miroir" (useless mirror) because they reflect no heaven. But when a herdsman comes to drink, although seemingly unaware of the sacredness of the spring, he is nevertheless performing "le geste héréditaire" (the hereditary act), an act repeated innumerable times and testifying to the transience of the individual human being and the permanence of forces transcending personal destinies.

In "Le Dieu Hêtre" the beech tree is deified. He is a familiar god protecting the simple and rustic life of the Gascons. When death comes to one of them, the tree, by supplying one of its branches for wood for the coffin, will continue to perform its protective role.

The last two sonnets in the group deify freedom as symbolized by mountains. For the slave Geminus in "Aux Montagnes divines" the rocky peaks with their glaciers, precipices and torrents, the pure and silent air of their summits, yield to no servile rule. To them, sacred guardians of liberty, he dedicates a cippus. Sabinula in "L'Exilée" also worships the nearby mountains and erects altars to them because their gods console her. An exile from Rome, she too has lost her freedom and, as she looks out over the mountains, she sees reflected in them the outlines of Rome.

Thus the creation of man-made monuments is one way in which man aspires to achieve some measure of permanence and perhaps also communication with the gods. Part of this role is explicitly expressed in "A un Triomphateur," where the emperor is exhorted to have someone sculpt rows of warriors, chiefs, armor, ships, names of families, and inscriptions of honors and titles "de peur que l'avenir te frustre" (for fear that the future may defraud you). But like man's dreams of glory and his acts of heroism, these artifacts are futile:

> Déjà le Temps brandit l'arme fatale. As-tu
> L'espoir d'éterniser le bruit de ta vertu?
> Un vil lierre suffit à disjoindre un trophée;

Already Time brandishes its fatal weapon. Do you hope to eternalize the message of your worth? A lowly vine is all it takes to split apart a trophy.

Time is man's mortal enemy and none of his efforts can eliminate his mortality, the prospect of which fleeting time makes so real. In fact, according to the speaker in "A Sextius" death is man's only certainty. It is merely the moment of its coming that is uncertain and comparable to the throw of the dice:

> . . . Mais la mort et ses funèbres fables
> Nous pressent, et, pour toi, seul le jour est certain
> Où les dés renversés en un libre festin
> Ne t'assigneront plus la royauté des tables.

But death and its funereal fables press us, and for you only that day is certain when the dice cast in an open feast no longer assign to you the royalty of the tables.

The transcience and fragility of individual human destinies stand out even more strongly against the background of the immutability of their setting. The thermal springs, the beech forest, and the mountains are some of the components of that setting. But man has not been able to shape any part of it in such a way as to leave any lasting trace of himself. As we see in "A un Triomphateur," even the lowly grass can frustrate his attempts to create any durable monument to his own glory:

> Et seul, aux blocs épars des marbres triomphaux
> Où ta gloire en ruine est par l'herbe étouffée,
> Quelque faucheur Samnite ébréchera sa faulx.

And against the scattered blocks of triumphal marble, where your glory in ruins is stifled by the grass, some solitary Samnite reaper will chip his scythe.

IV   The Middle Ages and the Renaissance

The third section of *Les Trophées* consists of twenty-five sonnets under the heading "Le Moyen Age et la Renaissance." Of these only the first three can be clearly linked with the Middle Ages, while the last eight carry the sub-title "Les Conquérants" (The Conquerors).

É-MARIA DE HEREDIA
nd in war. Their
by several cor-
s, sakers, the
ich occupied
heir crests,
with war.
h battle
y. The
The
the
all

enaissance poems seem to be
ek and Roman groups. It is
mainly from a different
themes, previously quite
or subordinated. Thus, the
of man and nature, nostalgia
he beauty of nature, the flight of
mication with the divine — none of
sition. As a whole this section gives the
n of looking to the past, but rather of looking
of presenting some vision of man's potentiality.
subject of this group of sonnets is superior human
ent, especially in the realm of art and artifacts. Except for
onnets devoted to the conquerors, in which human achievement
is less frequently manifested in the production of a concrete object,
almost every sonnet in the group is in some way connected with art
or craftsmanship. Their products include medals, swords, coins,
crests, coats of arms, stained glass windows, paintings, enamel work,
fine book bindings, epitaphs, tombs, verse, and work of carpenters
and goldsmiths. The image of man which emerges from these
poems, at least on the surface, is that of a dynamic and energetic being, confident that he can cope with his environment, leave his im-
print on it, and perpetuate something of himself in what he creates.
This image is of course compatible with our ideas of Renaissance
man. Many of Heredia's Renaissance sonnets are linked to that
period in history not only by this spirit but also by their reference to
events and historical figures of that time.

The first three sonnets in the group clearly belong to the Medieval
period. We can hardly expect to find in a mere forty-two verses
anything more than a few brief glimpses of some aspects of those
times, and yet the first of these sonnets gives a remarkable reproduc-
tion of their spirit as well as the most essential facets of their life. The
title of the sonnet, "Vitrail" (Stained glass window), is significant in
a number of ways. In the first place it is a man-made object which
outlasts man and on which he has recorded his deepest spiritual
values. As a window it serves as a vantage point from which feudal
society may be surveyed in a broad perspective; the poet says it has
seen ladies and barons. The window is the eye of the cathedral; it
reflects the fact that much of Medieval life was dominated by the
church and that the important moments of life converged in the
cathedral. Thus the feudal lords and ladies have bowed beneath the

consecrating hand of august priesthood in peace
life is recalled under those two broad categories
responding sets of terms. Their hoods, horns, falco
woods, and the flight of the herons suggest the hunt, w
much of their peace-time life. On the other hand,
bugles, swords, the plains, and the Crusades are linked
The reference to Constantinople and Saint John of Acre, b
sites during the Crusades, adds a note of historical authentici
finery and opulence of their clothing are briefly evoked as we
dominant character trait which emerges from this portrait is
feudal lords' pride. However, this type of self-importance appears
the more futile in the vision which the sestet presents. Here we se
their stone statues on their tombs. Whereas previously the pride o
these lords and ladies bowed only before the church, they now find
themselves in a lying position, silent, immobile, mute and sightless.
All their activities have ceased, and only the stone hounds on the
tombstone are left to recall what they used to do. And yet, in spite of
the brevity of their individual lives, the stone statues and the windows of the cathedral, both creations of man, represent an attempt to
preserve some trace of their lives.

The other two Medieval sonnets have their historical roots in the
time of Christ's life. "Epiphanie" presents the three Oriental kings,
Balthazar, Melchior and Caspar, as they journey at the head of a
long procession to the side of the Christchild, to whom they humbly
pay hommage and offer rich gifts. Heredia in this sonnet has tried to
capture something of the simplicity of early medieval faith. The
poem has the quality of a picture conceived by an unsophisticated
mind. In fact, Heredia alerts the reader to his intention by stating
that the three kings are "tels qu'ils sont dans les vieilles images" (as
they are in old pictures). Christ's mission is conceived in the simplest
terms; it is to cure the sufferings of man and animals. The familiar
side of his humanity is suggested when he responds to the kings with
gleeful laughter like any other baby.

The third Medieval sonnet, "Le Huchier de Nazareth," also deals
in a more familiar way with Christ's life. It presents a family scene in
which the most important members are referred to as "Madame la
Vierge," "Monseigneur Jésus" and "Saint Joseph." These forms of
address establish a "folksy" atmosphere. It is evening. Joseph and
Jesus have been doing carpentry all day in the workshop. Joseph,
very humanly, is tired but Jesus alone continues to work unabated,
thereby suggesting that he is no ordinary apprentice.

Heredia's concern with craftsmanship and human creativity is thus evident in his medieval poems and continues in his Renaissance sonnets. The objects of art in question are generally characterized by richness, durability and, less frequently, by more subtle, suggestive powers. It is almost entirely through such objects that the Renaissance is evoked. Frequent references to artists and artisans of the time and to events or people that inspired their work help to give the sonnets a ring of historical authenticity.

The first of the Renaissance sonnets, "L'Estoc," describes a sword made by the Spanish goldsmith Perez de Las Cellas for the Borgia family. Its richness and splendor, its sumptuous workmanship, and the family coat of arms including the papal insignia sum up better than words the spirit of this early Italian Renaissance era:

> Et ce glaive dit mieux qu'Arioste ou Sannazar,
> Par l'acier de sa lame et l'or de sa poignée,
> Le pontife Alexandre et le prince César.

And this sword expresses better than Ariosto or Sannazar through the steel of its blade and the gold of its hilt Pontiff Alexander and Prince Caesar.

"L'Epée" is another sonnet in which a sword is presented. Its fine craftsmanship is concisely described. Its hilt in the shape of Hercules testifies to Renaissance interest in antiquity. Julian del Rey, "prince of the forge," whose mark appears on the neck of the hilt, has succeeded in putting into the sword the essence of that haughty pride which has often been linked with Spanish nobility.

Like "L'Estoc," "Médaille" is also inspired by the early Italian Renaissance, an age of violence but also of erudition and culture. One of the striking figures of the time was Sigismond Malatesta de Rimini, whose profile appears on the medal struck by Matteo da Pasti, engraver, sculptor and goldsmith. The profile of Sigismond, which resembles that of a hawk, suggests his cruelty. The dual character of the age is represented by another medal, which inspired the last few verses of the sonnet. This second medal bears the profile of a smiling Isotta, Sigismond's wife, on one side, while the other shows an elephant, emblem of the family, trampling the primroses.

A number of other sonnets are also devoted to the plastic arts and crafts such as engraving, smithing, sculpting and enameling. "Sur le Pont-Vieux" can be regarded as a companion piece to "Le Huchier de Nazareth." Morning finds the master goldsmith in his workshop with his apprentices, but as the city of Florence comes to life most of the apprentices are distracted by the activities of the city. Only young Benvenuto Cellini, completely engrossed in his task, follows his inner vision as he engraves and sculpts the combat of the Titans on the handle of a dagger. "Le Vieil Orfèvre" presents an aging goldsmith, whose skill during his long career has matched or surpassed that of the best Spanish goldsmiths of the age. Now as he approaches death he hopes to assure his salvation by creating a golden monstrance, a Christian symbol, in place of the pagan objects to which he has devoted himself exclusively until now.

Heredia uses the language of the goldsmith even in "Vélin doré" to describe the fine binding of a sixteenth-century book with its gilt edge, gold work on its spine and delicate interlacing figures. Although the clear outlines of this embroidery have become faded with time, the book, once caressed by beautiful ladies, preserves and conveys through some mysterious charm the soul of their perfume and the shadow of their dream.

"A Claudius Popelin," "Email" and "Rêves d'Email" do not appear to have any obvious connection with the Renaissance. They form a group because all have to do with the enameler's art. The first one is dedicated to Heredia's friend, the enameler Claudius Popelin. In a sense the sonnet is three-tiered: artisans of the past have fixed various facets of the life of their times in their work; Popelin, their descendant and rival, perpetuates their sublime work; Heredia, in his turn, would wish his sonnet to be like Popelin's enamel work, crowning his friend with a wreath of glory. The other two sonnets cannot fail to recall parts of Gautier's "L'Art" relative to the enameler's art and to possible subject matter drawn from heraldic monsters. Heredia's two sonnets are in a large measure filled with suggestions for subjects to be treated. While a few of these come from medieval times, most of them are from antiquity, "le peuple monstrueux de la mythologie" (the monstrous characters of mythology).

In "La Dogaresse" Heredia has tried to reproduce the atmosphere of an Italian painting of the Venetian school. He suggests this in the opening verses by his reference to Titian:

> Le palais est de marbre où, le long des portiques,
> Conversent des seigneurs que peignit Titien . . . .

The palace is of marble, where along the porticos converse the lords whom Titian painted.

Heredia evokes the brilliant colors of the rich clothing worn by the proud noblemen and the opulence of the brocade gown of the dogaressa, who smiles at the little negro boy holding her train. But there is a static quality about the scene; the patricians looking out over the blue Adriatic and the lady turning toward the boy appear to be frozen against the hardness of the marble which forms the backdrop of the picture. Thus in a sense they are preserved as they were in life.

Three sonnets are concerned directly with poetry. They are inspired by the Renaissance poets Petrarch, Ronsard and du Bellay. "Suivant Pétrarque" recalls the style and subject matter of Petrarch. It evokes a young lady whose beauty is presented in a somewhat precious style through a comparison with the gold of the heavens dazzling the poor people. An admirer greets her but she rejects his attentions, albeit with just the right degree of hesitation so that he will not be completely discouraged. The sonnet inspired by Ronsard is entitled "Sur le Livre des Amours de Pierre de Ronsard." It begins with the thought that lovers throughout the ages have tried to preserve the record of their names, but death and the oblivion of the grave have triumphed over them all. The idea that even the beautiful bodies of our loves must end in dust finds a distant echo in Villon. However, that is not the fate of Marie, Hélène and Cassandre, the three ladies who inspired Ronsard's *Amours*, for Ronsard has immortalized them in his verse with a wreath of love and glory. In "La belle Viole" Heredia has succeeded in capturing something of the delicacy of du Bellay by combining in an ingenious manner reminiscences of a few well-known poems and themes of that poet. He plays with the word "viole," which we know to be the name of a girl who is considered to have inspired du Bellay's early collection of verse entitled *L'Olive*. The addition of a few letters in the fourth verse makes it a violet, while in the following verse it has the sense of "viol," the instrument she is playing. Du Bellay's love for his native Anjou is also recalled, as is the well known poem "D'un Vanneur de blé aux vents," from which the epigraph of the sonnet is taken. Perhaps the sonnet "Epitaphe" can also be attached to the three foregoing poems. Although not a poem in the usual sense, the epitaph in question is also an attempt to preserve a memory by means of a verbal construct. The sonnet was inspired by the epitaph prepared by Henry III for his friend and favorite Hyacinthe de Maugiron, killed in a duel by one of the followers of the Duc de Guise.

The eight sonnets under the sub-title "Les Conquérants" were inspired by the exploits of the Spanish *conquistadores*, who explored, conquered and colonized parts of the New World. A descendant of the conquistador Pedro de Heredia, José-Maria de Heredia must have taken a personal interest in this chapter of history, which in any event corresponded to his admiration for heroism and distinguished achievement. Although man-made objects are neither lacking nor unimportant in these sonnets, as we shall see, the foreground is occupied by adventure and the accomplishments and dreams of men of action.

The first sonnet, which gives its title to the whole group, may be regarded in some ways as a poetic condensation of Heredia's preface to his translation of Bernal Diaz's *Véridique histoire de la conquête de la Nouvelle-Espagne*. The sonnet, like the preface, tries to convey the tone and spirit of the times, and of the *conquistadores* in particular. It suggests a mentality made up, on the one hand, of a certain hard brutality, eagerness and greed for gold and, on the other hand, of a softer component, a dream of unknown mysteries and beauty which might await them in the distant West.

Most of the other sonnets in the group are devoted to the dreams and achievements of specific *conquistadores*. "Jouvence" tells of Ponce de Leon's search for a fountain of youth said to be located on one of the islands of the Bahamas. But instead of finding it he discovered Florida and founded a colony there. Thus, in a less literal sense, he did find a fountain of youth because his exploits have given him immortality. Hernando de Soto in "Le Tombeau du Conquérant," who among other things discovered the Mississippi, also attains a measure of immortality because the wind weeps and sings eternal prayers over his watery Mississippi grave, and because the river itself is his shroud.

The memory of the accomplishments of others is perpetuated by man-made objects, usually crests or coats of arms. Bartolomé Ruiz, prince of pilots, who contributed so much to the expansion of Castille's empire by guiding its fleets across the ocean to the New World, is remembered, "Carolo Quinto Imperante" tells us, in the royal coat of arms, where he is shown with an anchor. "L'Ancêtre," "A un Fondateur de ville" and "Au Même" all celebrate the accomplishments of Pedro de Heredia, an ancestor of the poet. The first of these reviews his exploits in claiming new land for Spain. The speaker contemplates Don Pedro's enamel portrait, produced by Claudius Popelin, to whom the poem is dedicated, and observes that it brings the distinguished ancestor back to life with his proud and melancholy character and his eyes which still seem to be seeking in the sky for further visions of the brilliance of New Spain. The other two sonnets concentrate on one of his specific achievements, the founding of the city of Carthagena in the West Indies. He wanted this city to be a proud monument to his race and to his own name. In "A un Fondateur de ville," however, we see that the city could not last and was no match for the permanence and strength of the ocean. Only the family crest with its city of silver shaded by a golden palm tree bears witness to the splendors of his dream. That is why, in "Au Même," his descendants also have put a golden palm tree shading a silvery city on their coat of arms, knowing that in this manner it will resist the erosive forces of time.

On the whole the Medieval and Renaissance sonnets express admiration for high achievement and confidence in the durability of man's best created objects, especially those that are hard, such as the ones produced by the enameler, the goldsmith and the engraver. In the Greek and Roman poems even marble could not resist the ravages of time. And if we look closely, even the Medieval and Renaissance sonnets, despite a certain air of confidence, are not free of an underlying feeling of melancholy, which perhaps issues from a realization of the ultimate vanity of all man's efforts and all his agitation. In the opening poem "Vitrail" all the activities of the most distinguished lords and ladies end in frozen and stony silence. The last sonnet "A une Ville morte," which once again evokes the city of Carthagena, this time its destruction by Sir Francis Drake, suggests that man's greatest ambitions are vain, especially compared to the mighty and eternal forces of nature. Man is doomed to silence:

> Et dans l'énervement des nuits chaudes et calmes,
> Berçant ta gloire éteinte, ô cité, tu t'endors
> Sous les palmiers, au long frémissement des palmes.

And in the enervating heat and calm of the nights, lulling to rest your extinguished glory, O city, you go to sleep beneath the palm trees, to the endless rustling of the palms.

V *The Orient and the Tropics*

"L'Orient et les Tropiques," the smallest section of *Les Trophées,* consists of nine sonnets, providing glimpses of ancient Egypt, feudal Japan and the splendor and luxuriance of selected scenes from

tropical nature. Some of these poems furnished Heredia the opportunity to reflect something of his own impressions of the color and
vegetation of the tropical setting in which he spent his earliest years.
In contrast to the preceding group of sonnets this one does not
emphasize man-made objects. Instead, some of the dominant
themes are a sense of the eternity and vastness of nature, the mystery
and beauty of life, and an underlying affirmation of life even in
death.

The Orient involved here is first of all Egypt. "La Vision de
Khèm," which opens "L'Orient et les Tropiques," is a cycle of three
sonnets. The first one, reminiscent of Leconte de Lisle's well known
"Midi," evokes the searing metallic heat of noon over Egypt, immobilizing man and beast alike. The bronze Anubis and the great
sphinxes in fact appear more animate than the living. This first scene
is followed by two nocturnal sonnets, closely linked, recreating a
landscape dominated by the moon over the Nile. The eerie effect of
the moonlight and its shadows makes it easy to imagine that forms
are changing shape and stirring. This is in fact what Khèm sees in his
vision, essentially that of a whole ancient necropolis coming to life.
All the sculpted granite forms begin to stir, to detach themselves
from the hieroglyph-covered walls, and to fall into place according
to a determined hierarchy in a procession that grows ever larger.
Even the sacred birds engraved on the tombs take flight, and the
sphinxes awaken with a start from their eternal sleep. The
hallucinatory character of the vision is emphasized by the total
absence of sound as the procession headed by the gods and including
the Pharaohs, their servants and animals winds through the ruined
temples. Although we can regard the scene as the strange effect
produced by the play of moonlight and shadows, and as a vision, we
may well ask whether it does not also represent the dream of
humanity generally to be immortal, to reawaken after the sleep of
death.

"Le Prisonnier" may also be attached to Heredia's Egyptian
poems, since its setting is once again the Nile. Dedicated to the
modern painter Gérôme, the sonnet attempts to capture some of the
pictorial qualities of Gérôme's "Le Prisonnier." An old Sheik is in
captivity on a boat. His two captors sit at opposite ends of the boat,
one lost in dreamy and drug-induced contemplation and the other
loudly taunting the prisoner, thereby insulting his human dignity.
The first quatrain paints a picture of the evening landscape, but the
prisoner, bound and restricted in his movements, can see only the

pointed minarets quivering in the Nile, a captured, limited landscape reflecting his own situation.

"Le Samouraï" and "Le Daïmio" present two aspects of feudal
Japanese warriors; the first poem concentrates on the lover and the
second on the heroic man of action. The Daïmio, or feudal prince, is
pictured in all his proud splendor, astride a fiery rearing stallion. It is
the morning of a battle and the disaster that is imminent contrasts
with the brilliance and cheeriness of the sun rising over the ocean
and illuminating the snowy volcano. As the prince contemplates this
splendor he raises his shield, on which appears the emblem of the rising sun, and we feel that he will try to respond to the glory of his
country with the bravery of his deeds. In "Le Samouraï" we also find
a portrait of a warrior in armor. With his metallic exterior, his shield,
his weapons, and his helmet, from which protrude two golden antennae, he reminds the poet of a crustacean. But he is not going to war.
The two antennae quivering on his helmet indicate his excitement,
for he has just seen his beloved, who has been waiting for him and
now sees him approaching, the victorious hero of her dreams.

Among the three "tropical" sonnets, "Fleurs de feu" and "Fleur
séculaire" belong together as companion pieces. Both evoke an old
volcanic mountain long extinct now, and in both a flower emerges
and grows out of this immobile volcanic soil. But each sonnet
emphasizes a different aspect of this growth, and thus the two complete one another. "Fleurs de feu" creates an impression of
timelessness and of the ageless earth. It recalls the beginnings, "Les
siècles du Chaos" (the centuries of Chaos), when the crater was like
a torrent of flame. Now it lies silent, cold and immobile; yet the ancient fire cannot be entirely suppressed, for through the powdery
rock bursts a cactus flower and scatters its pollen like a clap of
thunder in the midst of the silence. As we can see, the volcano with
its torrent of fiery lava is a fitting image of natural force and power.
But there is another force comparable to it, and that is the very principle of life, which will not be suppressed or denied. That is why,
even when it manifests itself as a lowly flower, the poet can speak of
it with the vocabulary that might describe the activity of a volcano.

We may recall that Heredia at one point considered choosing
"Fleurs de feu" as the title of the whole book of sonnets. That he
should have entertained such an idea is not surprising, since the
theme of the affirmation of life expressed in the sonnet characterizes
a substantial part of *Les Trophées*. Unfortunately Heredia could not
present this theme without reservations, for, although the forces of

life may be irrepressible, he realized that its individual manifestations are all too brief. This idea is incorporated in the companion sonnet "Fleur séculaire," which is at once so similar to "Fleurs de feu" and at the same time so different, like the other side of a medal. We find in it almost the same components as in the other sonnet. The flower, an aloe this time, grows, finally blooms, and its giant pistil scatters its pollen explosively over a wide area. But the last few verses suggest the melancholy thought that, after all, the beauty of the flower is only brief:

> Et le grand aloès à la fleur écarlate,
> Pour l'hymen ignoré qu'a rêvé son amour,
> Ayant vécu cent ans, n'a fleuri qu'un seul jour.

And the large aloe with its scarlet flower, having lived a hundred years, bloomed but a single day for the unknown marriage of which its love dreamed.

The Oriental and Tropical section closes with "Le Récif de Corail," which might be described as a virtuoso piece in which Heredia captures something of the feeling of the mysteries of marine life in the depths of the ocean. He is especially successful in conveying the effects of ever-changing and coruscating color and movement in these depths. With a final brush stroke he pictures a large fish slowly floating among the mosses, algae, anemones and coral. A sudden movement of its fins changes the visual effect, transforming the crystalline blue of the water into a jewel-like pattern of gold, mother-of-pearl and emeralds.

VI *Nature and Dream*

The last group of sonnets in *Les Trophées* is called "La Nature et le Rêve." Whereas the first three groups of sonnets have a fairly distinct chronological and historical orientation, this is less clear in the last two. On the whole, however, the setting of "La Nature et le Rêve" appears to be Brittany as Heredia knew it in the nineteenth century. Most of the poems by far in this section are inspired by the Breton landscape or seascape. Ten of them, under the sub-heading "La Mer de Bretagne," are dedicated to the painter Emmanuel Lansyer, who was a friend of Heredia.

The title "La Nature et le Rêve" is suggestive of the character of the sonnets under it. While we find in them most of the themes from previous groups, the emphasis, as in each of the other groups, is once again different. In no other group does the landscape play such a large part. Dream represents the human element. Perhaps it suggests also a more imaginative, more lyrical and more personal attitude on the part of Heredia. In any case nature and dream encompass the most fundamental aspects of existence, man and nature. Nature is presented not solely as a landscape or object apart from man. Man in the presence of nature constitutes a confrontation between the ephemeral and the immutable, the mortal and the ageless. Nature is a mirror in which man sees the image of strength and immortality to which he aspires; but nature is also an image of the profound and hidden mysteries of existence, and in that sense Heredia suggests, more than in any other part of *Les Trophées*, the fraternity between it and man, which stems from obscurely felt, primordial bonds of union between the two.

"La Nature et le Rêve" opens with three sonnets which might have been included among the Greek and Sicilian poems; all three had in fact appeared in that context in the *Parnasse contemporain* of 1876. In all three we find echoes of antiquity. However, whereas in the Greek and Sicilian section Heredia evokes antiquity without reference to the present, he emphasizes in these three sonnets the contrast between the past and the present. The vantage point of the present allows us to see what changes the passing of time has effected.

The first of these three sonnets, "Médaille antique," recalls Gautier's lines,

> Tout passe. — L'Art robuste
> Seul a l'éternité.

> All things pass away. — Robust art alone has eternity.

The maidens whose grace Theocritus evoked no longer exist. Arethusa is no longer pure, the Sicilian city of Agrigente is only a shadow and Syracuse seems dead under the blue shroud of the sky. Even marble shows wear. Only the hard metal of the silver medallions immortalizes the beauty of the Sicilian maidens. Meanwhile, nature itself has not changed, and Mount Etna still nourishes the grapes on its slopes as it did during the time of Theocritus.

"Les Funérailles" laments the passing of an age of glory. When warriors of Greek antiquity died they were recognized by the whole country, and even the forces of nature appeared to notice. But now, says the speaker, he will die an old man and be put into a coffin and someone will have to pay for the burial plot, the priest and the candles. Yet, instead of such a prosaic fate, he too has dreamed of a more glorious destiny, of dying young, a hero's death, like his ancestors. "Vendange" also presents a confrontation between the "yesterday" and the "today." The scene of a grape harvest, reminiscent of Lamartine's "La Vigne et la Maison," recalls to the poet the Bacchanalian wine celebrations of antiquity, but today the landscape is no longer inhabited by divinities. Still not everything is changed; the grape harvest takes place under the same sky that witnessed the Bacchanalian revels and autumn still interweaves the black tresses and the golden mane of the vines, thus perpetuating the age-old sense of the mystery of existence and of the sameness of man's dreams.

Between the poems of antiquity and the Breton poems we find the sonnet "La Sieste," whose verbal virtuosity reminds us of "Le Récif de Corail." It evokes the drowsy heat of noon, the silence, the dense vegetation, and the lace-work pattern of the light rays filtering through the foliage. The only movement in the scene is the flight of the butterflies intoxicated by the light and the perfume. In this atmosphere the speaker actively tries to imprison his dreams in the lacy network of the light, thus incorporating them in the subtle designs of nature.

The sub-section "La Mer et la Bretagne" consists of ten sonnets devoted to the Breton landscape and the sea. It is a very old land, recalling ancient clans and legends of dwarfs and demons. The menhirs rising into the somber sky like stony cypresses mark the tombs of the brave of long ago and emphasize man's mortality in contrast to the unchanging landscape, "l'homme immobile auprès de l'immuable chose" (immobile man in the presence of immutable things), as Heredia so aptly puts it in "Bretagne." The land itself is flat, grey and monotonous. The soil is hard. The eye sees vast expanses of furze and heather broken sometimes by hedges and houses covered by vines and ivy. Other aspects of the landscape are fields of grain and the moors with their valleys, from which come the distant sounds of the herdsmen as they bring back the cattle in the evening. There is a ruggedness about the land and a wildness in the odor of the furze. Those who belong to it delight in the freedom of its open spaces and the splendors of its ruggedness. They are like the shepherd in "Armor," who, making a sweeping gesture with his arms, proclaims with a certain possessive pride that this is Armorica. Perhaps the most striking aspect of the Breton land is that it is almost everywhere dominated by the ocean. Striking also are the many faces of the sea and the astonishing variety of ways in which Heredia has evoked it. "Un Peintre," which is the first sonnet in the Breton cycle, forms a fitting introduction to the group. In stating what the painter has done it announces what the poet will be doing as well:

> Il a peint l'Océan splendide, immense et triste,
> Où le nuage laisse un reflet d'améthyste,
> L'émeraude écumante et le calme saphir;
>
> Et fixant l'eau, l'air, l'ombre et l'heure insaisissables,
> Sur une toile étroite il a fait réfléchir
> Le ciel occidental dans le miroir des sables.

He has painted the ocean splendid, immense and sad, where the clouds leave a reflection of amethyst, the foaming emerald and the calm sapphire; and fixing the water, the air, the shadows and the intangible hour on a narrow canvas, he has made the mirror of the sands reflect the western sky.

The foregoing sonnet gives us some idea of the complexity of Heredia's conception of the sea. He pictures it both in its stormy and its calm moments; he shows it to be splendid and monstrous, consoling and dangerous; he makes us perceive it visually, but also through smell and hearing; and he emphasizes its immensity, immutability and timeless mystery.

In most of these poems Heredia prefers to present the sea at sunset, or at least in the evening. That is the time when the splendor of the sun's colors can best unite with that of the ocean, either turbulent and foamy, or calm. It is also the time when shadows begin to gather, obscuring the boundaries separating land, sky and water, and thus creating a vision of endless space such as we find, for example, in "Armor":

> Et mon coeur savoura, devant l'horizon vide
> Que reculait vers l'Ouest l'ombre immense du soir,
> L'ivresse de l'espace et du vent intrépide.

And before the empty horizon, which the immense evening shadows were pushing toward the West, my heart savored the intoxication of space and of the intrepid wind.

"Soleil couchant" creates an atmosphere of nocturnal harmony,
peace and unity, whose character takes on a religious tone as the
angelus unites with the sound of the sea. At the horizon the dying
sun "sur un ciel riche et sombre,/Ferme les branches d'or de son
rouge éventail" (against a rich and sombre sky closes the golden
branches of its red fan). All is silent now, save the vast murmur of the
ocean. In "Floridum mare" land and sea merge through an ingenious interchange of character. The fields of grain with their un-
dulating movement become an ocean, while the sea with its sunset
colors becomes an immense meadow of green and of multi-colored
flowers. To complete this interchange, the sea gulls follow the tide
toward the land, while the butterflies flutter over the "flowering
ocean."

The sunset landscape in "Blason céleste" unites sea and sky. The
virtuosity and imaginative powers which Heredia displays here
recall those of Victor Hugo's *Orientales*. He sees the sky as a celestial
stained glass window on which the sun and changing clouds produce
the effect of a huge heraldic shield against the blue enamel of the
sky. The shifting cloud formations at first suggest heraldic monsters
and giants in combat, and then celestial battles between demonic
Seraphim and Archangels. This prehuman epic is followed by a
reference to the Medieval crusades, and finally, in the framework of
the present, we glimpse again the heraldic shield now composed of
the green background of the sea and the golden bezant of the sun.

The Breton sea is not only splendid, but also monstrous, as
Heredia says in "Armor." It is not always like a "calm sapphire";
sometimes it is a "foaming emerald," and sometimes, as in "Un
Peintre," its churning whiteness makes us think of a sheep's wool. In
its stormy moments it vents its fury on the craggy granite cliffs. In
"Mer montante" the voice of the waves exploding with misty spray
against the reefs is like rumbling thunder, and their foamy crests
make us think of huge sea monsters. The fearful aspects of the Atlantic are underlined in "Maris stella," where the wives of fishermen in-
voke the holy star, their plaintive prayer rising above the clamor of
the sea. They look toward the north, where their men have gone, and
see the churning ocean. As in Hugo's "Oceano Nox," they are
keenly aware of the dangers of the sea and they realize that many
brave fishermen will not come back.

Yet the ocean can also comfort and refresh. The salty odor borne
by the winds from the water and the seaweed is almost like a perfume. When the lungs are filled with this air, the heart is uplifted.

"Le Bain," especially, conveys such an invigorating effect. In it a rider and his stallion plunge into the icy Atlantic. The spray hits their skin, the swells rise like walls, and man and beast breathe in the odor of salt water. The stallion neighs as it rears, while the rider, hair flying in the wind, shouts his delight as together making up a statuesque figure they savor the joy of freedom and challenge.

Deep and mysterious bonds unite man and the ocean. The low murmur of the sea responds to man's sadness and comforts his heavy heart ("Bretagne"). In "Mer montante" this fraternity is even more evident. The speaker, contemplating the violent sea, finds in himself also a flood of thoughts, dreams, hopes and spent strength, leaving only a bitter memory. The sound of the ocean, however, is for him a fraternal voice because it is like the eternal lament of mankind rising toward God in vain.[6] On a very personal level for Heredia, the sea has a special meaning in "Brise marine." The boundless waters of the Atlantic breaking against the Breton shore are also those surrounding the blue Antilles three thousand leagues away. As he smells the Atlantic air a warmth fills his heart and the air seems strangely perfumed. He recognizes in it the fragrance of his native island. The ocean thus unites him with his past and his homeland.

The transition from the sonnets of "La Mer de Bretagne" to the remaining ones is made by "La Conque," which in a sense takes up with variations the theme of "Mer montante." We find again the notion of the eternal complaint of the sea. The seashell, after having been buffeted by the waves for many a winter, is destined to hear forever within itself the moaning of the sea. Just as the shell has imprisoned the voice of the sea eternally, so in the speaker's heart there is the low, eternal, distant and stormy sound of the soul, whose mysterious music can be represented by the image of the ocean's distant and timeless lament. "La Conque" is followed by "Le Lit," a sonnet which expresses the idea that a bed, of whatever quality it may be, is the scene of the key moments of man's earthly life: birth, rest, marital union, and death.

The remaining sonnets return to Heredia's concerns, found so often in *Les Trophées*, with superior achievement, heroism, death, and the quest for immortality. "La Mort de l'aigle" is a variation on the myth of Icarus. Like Leconte de Lisle's condor or Baudelaire's albatross, the eagle is solitary and wishes to escape from terrestrial shackles to higher zones corresponding to more lofty aspirations; but as it rises toward the sun and a clearer sky, it is struck by lightning and plunges earthward. Yet is is fortunate, for to die in the cause of

liberty and honor in the fullness of strength and in the pursuit of an
ideal is a glorious death. In "Plus ultra" the speaker is also consumed
by a thirst for new accomplishments and unheard-of discoveries. He
is tired of the "easy glory" of the *conquistadores* and eager to climb
the furthest promontories and to overcome all obstacles in reaching
the unknown polar seas, which will respond to his pride with their
"murmur of glory."

Two other sonnets have to do with superior achievement in the
arts. "Au Tragédien E. Rossi" eulogizes the Italian actor Ernesto
Rossi, whom Heredia had heard in Milan in 1864 and again three
years later together with his wife in Venice. The actor's perfor-
mances of Shakespearean roles run the gamut of human emotions
but it is when he reads some of Dante's *Inferno* that the poet has a
vision of a world beyond the human one. Hell becomes a reality and
he can almost feel the red reflection of the infernal flames. In
"Michel-Ange" we find a related idea; like Shakespeare,
Michelangelo heard in his inner being the voice of human emotions.
Promethean figure that he was, he felt chained to the highest summits, realizing the vanity of human ideals: "Il songeait que tout
meurt et que le rêve ment." (He was thinking that everything dies
and that dreams are illusory.) And yet in his painting he has
transmitted the fire of his proud soul to the cold marble of the
chapel, and has captured the terror of God's wrath on the day of the
Last Judgment.

In a sense "La Vie des morts" is also related to achievement in the
arts, but its emphasis is on the idea of immortality. Dedicated to
Heredia's friend, the poet Armand Silvestre, this sonnet evokes three
distinct images of immortality. In the first quatrain Heredia envisages the rebirth of himself and Silvestre, their bodies coming to
life again in the lily and the rose. The middle section of the poem
pictures death as a celestial and interstellar voyage, an ascent toward
the sun, where their souls will unite and be engulfed "in the felicity
of the eternal flames." The final image of immortality, reminiscent
of some of Heredia's Greek poems and not without a certain Ronsardian flavor, is one that is conferred by glory:

> Cependant que sacrant le poète et l'ami,
> La Gloire nous fera vivre à jamais parmi
> Les Ombres que la Lyre a faites fraternelles.

Meanwhile, celebrating the poet and the friend, Glory will make us live
forever among the Shades which the Lyre has made fraternal.

"La Nature et le Rêve" closes with the sonnet "Sur un marbre brisé." It evokes the marble figure of a god. It is just as well that its eyes are overgrown with moss, for the age of divine worship is over. It would look in vain for a maiden to offer libations of milk and wine. The statue's head is overgrown with vegetation and it is mutilated to such an extent that it is unrecognizable. But the oblique rays of the sun light up its eyes and the grape vines become red lips. A miracle has occurred: the sun and the breeze have given light and movement to transform the statue into a living god. But the change is only brief, an illusion of life, like a momentary glimmer of hope. Once again the vanity of man's activities has been underlined. His work, even on the hardest of materials, does not last. Neither have the gods endured. Only nature remains, an unchanged vital force.

VII   *The "Romancero" and the "Conquérants de l' or"*

"La Nature et le Rêve" is followed first by the "Romancero," composed of three longer poems entitled "Le Serrement des mains," "La Revanche de Diego Laynez," and "Le Triomphe du Cid," and then by a lengthy poem in six parts entitled "Les Conquérants de l'or." The "Romancero" and the "Conquérants de l'or" appear to be an appendix rather than an integral part of *Les Trophées*. It is likely that Heredia originally wanted his book to consist only of sonnets; we may recall that he told Pierre Louÿs that the trophies were his sonnets. However, his feeling that he did not have enough sonnets together with the lack of time to complete some of his unfinished ones may have influenced him to add these longer poems. Furthermore, their subject matter, the heroism of the Spanish Renaissance, was very close to his heart.

His source for the "Romancero" was the *Romancero général ou Recueil des chants populaires de l'Espagne*, a translation by Delahays, published in 1844.[7] It deals with the adventures of the Cid, of which the best known version in French is, of course, Corneille's play *Le Cid*. In Heredia's interpretation the aging Diego Laynez, humiliated by an affront from Don Gomez, and too old to restore the family honor, puts his sons to the test of squeezing their hands in his vise-like grip. The youngest, Ruy Diaz (Rodrigo), later to be known as the Cid, reacts in the most worthy manner and is chosen to avenge his father. Soon afterward Rodrigo returns with the head of Don Gomez. Thus having avenged his father, he is allowed to sit at a place of honor at the table, for, says his father, with a play on the word "chef," "qui porte un tel chef est Chef de ma maison" (whoever bears such a head is Head of my house). Some time later he returns with his army, victorious over the infidels. As the king is about to receive him, a woman suddenly appears asking the king for vengeance because the Cid has killed her father. She is Chimène Gomez. The king, recognizing the validity of her claim, hesitates and then proposes that she marry the Cid, a solution she accepts.

Heredia does not follow his model slavishly; he shortens the narrative, occasionally adds details, and sometimes changes events in time or place.[8] The effect is to heighten the drama and the epic quality of the story. He is not so much interested in its tragic or psychological aspects. Furthermore he succeeds in maintaining its Spanish flavor, so much so that his "Romancero" has been labeled more Spanish than the Spanish version.[9]

What Heredia placed under the heading "Les Conquérants de l'or" is really only the prologue of a much longer poem which he at one time envisaged. The subject was one which intrigued him and with which he no doubt felt emotional ties because one of his ancestors had been a *conquérant* of some importance. His sonnet "Les Conquérants," first published in 1869, two years before "Les Conquérants de l'or," was followed by several others also devoted to the Spanish conquerors of the New World and taking their place in the section "Le Moyen Age et la Renaissance." Perhaps Heredia felt the desire to treat the subject again in a different verse form in order to escape from the constraints of the sonnet and thus achieve a greater epic scope. It may be well to recall at this point also that the first volume of his four-volume translation of Bernal Diaz's account of the conquest of New Spain came out in 1877. Certainly in this undertaking Heredia must have experienced the satisfaction of being free to work with detailed and vast canvases. It may be that he decided not to complete "Les Conquérants de l'or" because his prose work was in fact the large epic of the *conquistadores* which he had envisaged, and which thus filled the role originally planned for the poem.

The poem "Les Conquérants de l'or" as we have it in *Les Trophées* is a rhymed chronicle of the events leading to the moment when Pizarro solemnly takes possession of Peru in 1534 in the name of Emperor Charles V. It begins with a sketch of the background of Pizarro's expeditions. Balboa has discovered the Pacific, and there is a general feeling that gold and other wealth are to be found on the Pacific shores of South America. Preliminary failures underline the dangers of exploratory ventures and the need for a strong leader. In

November, 1524, Pizarro sets out. The hardships he encounters are set forth in graphic detail. Some of his men force him to turn back, but he returns later with the pilot Bartolomé Ruiz. Heredia evokes the exotic splendors of the tropical coast. The explorers see the volcanic Chimborazo and Cotopaxi and finally come upon the town of Tumbez in a gulf, where they gather some gold and other gifts to take back to the emperor in Spain. Here Pizarro finally gains the emperor's support for further expeditions.

Ennobled and honored, he sets out once again, this time with the object of penetrating into the interior beyond Tumbez. In Tumbez he learns of a civil war among the Incas and of the victory of the chieftain Atahualpa. Heredia describes the arduous ascent of the Andes, which takes five months. At this point, as Pizarro and his followers are ready for the descent of the western slopes, Heredia describes in great detail the 106 footmen and the 62 hidalgo horsemen that make up the expedition. The leaders and the most distinguished hidalgos are named and identified. Their accomplishments, dress, weapons, crests, even their horses, are described in a manner reminiscent of some of the Medieval epics. The picture has a heroic grandeur, which may appear surprising for a poet so accustomed to working within the limits of the sonnet. The same epic breadth is maintained in the next and final part of the poem, where the descent of the expedition takes place. The majestic peaks of the Andes behind them and the sweeping plains covered by the tents of the Incas in front of them produce an unrivaled panorama as the setting sun projects its long rays over the scene. At this moment, when his followers are still mesmerized by the sight, Pizarro proudly plants the banner in the Peruvian soil and takes possession of it in the name of Don Carlos, the emperor. The heroism of the men and the glory of Spain are magnificently underlined by the splendor of the dying sun:

> Alors, formidable, enflammée
> D'un haut pressentiment tout entière, l'armée,
> Brandissant ses drapeaux sur l'occident vermeil,
> Salua d'un grand cri la chute du Soleil.

Then, formidable, enflamed with elevated foreboding, the army all together, brandishing their flags toward the scarlet west, greeted the setting sun with a loud cry.

CHAPTER 5

An Elegiac Perfume

A S we have seen, *Les Trophées* range over many centuries, from Greek cosmology to nineteenth-century Brittany. In this respect they are, however, not unique in nineteenth-century French literature. The epic has always been a prestigious genre in French literature, and many a French writer has dreamed of producing a great epic composition. But I think we may agree that the genre was not too successful between the best of the Medieval *Chansons de geste* and the end of the eighteenth century. In the nineteenth century the epic experienced a new birth, not only in the large number of epics that were produced, but also in the conception of its character and form.[1] Indeed, the latter tended to be somewhat amorphous; advances in scientific thought, history and philology led to new approaches, and the more traditional notion that an epic had to be national was often replaced by the more grandiose ambition of presenting in part or in its entirety the story of mankind. Many nineteenth-century writers, major as well as minor ones, undertook such a project. Sometimes their excessive ambition forced them to leave their work unfinished. Lamartine, for example, wrote only two episodes of his *Visions*, a work which was to be "grand comme le temps et le monde" (as large as time and the world).

The earliest of the major nineteenth-century French writers to attempt to give an image of mankind through the evocation of past civilizations from the perspective of poetized history was Chateaubriand in *Les Natchez* and *Les Martyrs*. Other major Romantics who attempted the epic were Lamartine, Vigny and Hugo. Among minor writers, Auguste Barbier in his *Rimes héroïques* of 1843 and perhaps even in his earlier *Il Pianto* was one of the first to write a cyclical epic in sonnet form. Most of the Parnassian poets followed the practice of producing small epics in cyclical groupings. The epic of humanity thus became almost a commonplace in the nineteenth century.

I *The Examples of Hugo and Leconte de Lisle*

Two of the best known examples of works in verse, taken from the second half of the century and devoted to the history of mankind or to aspects of its history, are Hugo's *La Légende des siècles* and most of the poems in the four collections published by Leconte de Lisle. A brief consideration of these two important models may help to place Heredia's *Trophées* in clearer perspective. Victor Hugo was, after all, probably the most prestigious French poet of the century and his *Légende des siècles* was the prototype of the kind of French epic composed of a large number of individual poems rather than consisting of one sustained poem. Most of Leconte de Lisle's poetry also constitutes a "legend of the ages," the best known of those produced by the Parnassians.

La Légende des siècles, which appeared in three series beginning in 1859, was to be an epic of humanity, showing it in its various aspects throughout the ages. In fact Hugo's aim was even more ambitious; he envisaged a trilogy in which *Dieu* (God) and *La Fin de Satan* (The End of Satan), neither one completed, would be added to the *Légende* to form a vast cosmic epic of existence. *Dieu* reviews conceptions of God and man's progress in his attempts to know and define His essence. *La Fin de Satan* is the denouement of the struggle between good and evil, spirit and matter, a struggle from which humanity and the cosmos will be delivered when evil ceases to exist after God finally pardons Satan.

The epic qualities of *La Légende des Siècles* are unmistakable. Although its real hero is man in a general sense, we find in it numerous poems devoted to historical and legendary figures, some already larger than life, but magnified still further by Hugo. Many of the events narrated are extraordinary, and their settings are characterized by a sense of grandeur. Hugo's own strength of imagination, propensity for exaggeration and above all prodigious visionary power provide a sense of the supernatural and a heightened feeling of life and vitality residing at the very heart of even inanimate objects.

The scenes from the history of mankind as Hugo has chosen them are hardly representative enough to satisfy a historian. Nor does his documentation save historical accuracy from anachronisms, prej-

udices, personal preferences and even outright invention to conceal
gaps in knowledge. To history he adds legend and apocalypse as
allies. But his personality dominates everything. As he takes us down
the path of history, from earliest times to a visionary twentieth century, we notice that this epic has a central thread or thesis, which is
briefly the gradual ascent of mankind as the forces of light and spirit
triumph over those of darkness and matter.

Hugo's conception of the poet as prophet, seer and leader of
humanity is well known. As a leader among his contemporaries he
was very much a man of his century. He shared the belief, widely
held since the eighteenth century, in the perfectibility and progress
of man and his condition. It was from this point of view that he
treated history and legend in his epic. That is why he did not really
succeed in making himself the contemporary of the civilizations he
resurrects, why his medieval episodes, for example, have a romantic
coloring and why his own inventions were sometimes necessary
when historical fact did not conform to his thesis.

But fortunately, the vaunted objectivity and erudition of the Parnassians would provide a more historically accurate evocation of past
civilizations in Leconte de Lisle's poetry. If, on the whole, this is
true, that is not to say that historical accuracy necessarily leads to
better poetry. While I think that Leconte de Lisle's erudition is
superior to Hugo's and that he is less prone to anachronisms, he also
is obsessed with an idea, in a sense the reverse of Hugo's. Whereas
Hugo has a vision of progress, Leconte de Lisle sees uninterrupted
regression after the age of Greek civilization, detests his own age,
and envisages the only acceptable solution as the complete destruction of the universe, ending in total oblivion.

Leconte de Lisle's poems, aside from some descriptive and lyric
ones, are a "legend of the centuries" in the sense that they evoke
religions and mythologies of past civilizations. Although he covers a
wide range of civilizations, it is impossible for him, as for Hugo, to
include all of them. If for Leconte de Lisle the Hellenic Age is the
preferred one, the modern era beginning with the Middle Ages is the
most hated one. In presenting a procession of religious creeds, each
relevant for a time and each supplanted by a successor, he is adding
nothing basically new to nineteenth-century thought. However,
what is more particularly his own contribution is not only to show
that the Christian church and the Christian God had replaced and
destroyed various pagan and polytheistic creeds, but also, and especially, to vent his resentment and anger with great vehemence

upon the church for having replaced creeds which existed in times which he considered more poetic, more beautiful and more nearly conforming to his vision of paradise.

His stated requirement that the poet should make himself the contemporary of the epoch which he wishes to evoke thus not only serves the cause of historical authenticity but also, I suspect, reflects his personal preference for the past and his aversion to the present. Both his and Hugo's epic poems contain unforgettable heroic figures and passages of great narrative power. But Leconte de Lisle is, if anything, less detached emotionally than Hugo. His main thesis or unifying idea is, in fact, less an idea than a feeling. Hugo's, on the other hand, is less an idea than a vision.

II *History versus Art*

While Heredia was writing in the shadows of these two prestigious poets, Hugo, whom he admired from a distance, and Leconte de Lisle, with whom he worked closely, he elaborated his own version of a "legend of the centuries" in *Les Trophées*. Aside from the obvious difference that this book is composed of sonnets, it appears, on the surface at least, not to be so different in conception. It contains heroic characters, sometimes presents events of epic dimensions, and offers glimpses of scenes through history from Greek times to Modern times.

We find that Heredia sees in the various historical epochs and civilizations a succession of changing settings in which the fundamental identity of man through the ages may be sought. One of his own pronouncements appears to confirm such a view of history:

Depuis les premiers jours du monde, l'homme, toujours le même, mû par les mêmes passions atroces, viles ou sublimes, s'agite dans la nature immuable. Divers par la race, il est semblable par les instincts. Mais les nécessités de la vie, la lutte pour l'existence, la défense contre la mort, l'ont diversement, suivant les climats et les âges, armé ou vêtu. La religion, les arts de la guerre et de la paix ont modifié sa forme extérieure, l'attitude, le geste.[2]

From the first days of the world, man, always the same, moved by the same passions, atrocious, base or sublime, flounders about in immutable nature. Diverse by race, he is the same by instincts. But the necessities of life, his struggle for existence, his defence against death, have armed or clothed him differently according to climate or era. Religion and the arts of war and peace have modified his external form, his attitudes, his gestures.

In order to present these various ages, the artist, according to
Heredia, must have in him a feeling for the life of each age, trying,
as Leconte de Lisle did, to make himself the contemporary of it. This
requires patient study and erudition. Heredia cannot be found wanting in this respect. His personal library was large and varied. He
knew Oriental literatures and read dictionaries, bibliographies and
catalogues, digesting material thoroughly. Factual errors are even
rarer in *Les Trophées* than in Leconte de Lisle's poetry. He consulted not only printed documents but also specialists in many fields,
especially the various crafts which play such an important role in his
sonnets, notably those of the Renaissance.

But Heredia did not consider documentation and erudition to be
sufficient. It was necessary further to have a kind of archetypal vision which would allow the poet to identify with the figures he was
resurrecting from the distant past, to feel what they felt, to see what
they saw; in short, to have a mysterious and almost intuitive insight
into their lives. He explains his attempts to achieve this in his own
work as follows:

J'ai essayé tour à tour de me faire l'âme d'Hercule, de me mettre dans la
peau d'Hercule, de sentir comme une nymphe, de devenir le berger de
Grèce qui "attache à ce vieux tronc moussu la brebis pleine," l'esclave de
Syracuse, né libre et songeant à revoir les yeux de sombre violette de celle
qu'il aime, de voir ces yeux si purs sourire au ciel natal qui s'y reflète, sous
l'arc victorieux que tend un sourcil noir.[3]

I tried in turn to make my soul that of Hercules, to put myself into the skin
of Hercules, to feel like a nymph, to become the Greek shepherd who "ties
the full sheep to this old mossy trunk," the slave of Syracuse, born free and
dreaming of seeing again the dark violet eyes of the one he loves, of seeing
those eyes, so pure, smiling at his native sky reflected by them beneath the
victorious arch of a dark eyebrow.

The impression that emerges from Heredia's approach is that art
regularly takes precedence over history. The fact that he undertook
to evoke past civilizations can be attributed only partly to a general
renaissance of historical erudition in the nineteenth century or to his
own academic training and interest in history. History was for him
only a tool serving what he considered to be the higher aims of art;
his use of history was inseparable from his conception of poetry. Like
so many of his Parnassian contemporaries, he found in history a
means of keeping his poetry impersonal. But perhaps the basic ele-

ment of his poetic creed was that poetry had to do with what was permanent and eternal, not with the ephemeral, the contemporary. In order to capture this sense of the eternal, the poet had to turn to the past in his quest for knowledge of the essence of man and life. Real poetry was not to be confused with the outward trappings of an age but had its roots in what was primitive and basic. Perhaps the notion that the past is poetic was a heritage left by the Romantics. Indeed it is with regard to Lamartine that Heredia sets forth his basic ideas; after having condemned public confession by poets, he cites Lamartine as a man of genius who was one of those rare men to whom the right of such confessions might be accorded. And yet even he generalized and idealized his intimate feelings. This remark leads to the following statement:

C'est que la vraie poésie est dans la nature et dans l'humanité éternelles et non dans le coeur de l'homme d'un jour, quelque grand qu'il soit. Elle est essentiellement simple, antique, primitive et, pour cela, vénérable. Depuis Homère, elle n'a rien inventé, hormis quelques images neuves pour peindre ce qui a toujours été. Le poète est d'autant plus vraiment et largement humain qu'il est plus impersonnel.[4]

It is because true poetry is in eternal nature and humanity and not in the heart of the man of one day, however great he may be. It is essentially simple, ancient, primitive and therefore venerable. Since Homer it has invented nothing outside of a few new images to depict what has always been. The poet is all the more truly and broadly human the more impersonal he is.

We should therefore not expect to find in *Les Trophées* a history of humanity in the ordinary sense. As history this collection would be open to grave criticisms. We could charge Heredia with omitting important periods, with providing no place at all for certain civilizations, such as the Nordic ones and India among others, and perhaps even with giving insufficient attention to the history of France.[5] Furthermore, the work is dominated by no obvious unifying historical thesis. Perhaps the most serious defect would be that the historical material seems to have been chosen almost at random, much in the manner of a man who takes a leisurely stroll and stops now and then in front of some object which catches his eye and pleases him. These scenes, although taken from history, do not always represent its most significant moments and are sometimes repetitious, as for example the numerous sonnets devoted to Renaissance crafts. History for Heredia is very much like a museum filled with trophies linked with man's achievements and whose deeper significance in the framework of existence the poet seeks to illuminate.

III Trophies of Humanity

The title itself may have been suggested by two sixteenth-century collections of sonnets, *Les Trophées du roy* by Jean Godart and *Les Trophées de la foi* by Du Bartas. Its meaning gives an indication of what we can expect in the book. For his daughter it represents a "choix de quelques emblèmes privilégiés parmi le butin de l'érudition et des rêves, des siècles et des races, des fables et des dieux, des empires et des êtres"[6] (choice of a few privileged emblems from among the spoils of erudition and dream, of centuries and races, of fables and gods, of empires and beings). It is important to keep in mind the basic meaning of trophies as spoils of victory or as artistic representations of objects symbolic of victory or achievement.

It is this meaning, I think, that applies to Heredia's sonnets in the sense that they are monuments dedicated to mankind's victories and achievements. We may consider Heredia's trophies as multi-tiered and mutually reinforcing. On one level Heredia chooses scenes representing distinguished human achievement. On another, he evokes monuments, works of art and other man-made trophies commemorating such achievements or intended to preserve traces of man's activities and creeds. Finally, embracing these two, are Heredia's sonnets themselves, trophies meant to protect some of the finest moments of mankind from oblivion. To give one concrete example, we may take "A un Fondateur de ville." Here we find first a reference to the exploits of a *conquistador*, one of which is the founding of Carthagena as a monument to preserve the memory of his name, and then an evocation of a silver heraldic crest bearing witness to his splendid dreams. At the same time the sonnet itself is a monument perpetuating the memory of those accomplishments.

This conception of *Les Trophées* implies a certain view of existence. For Heredia, as perhaps for Leconte de Lisle also, the cult of beauty and the enjoyment of art were supreme. Whereas the older poet, strongly attracted to the more passive and contemplative creeds of the Far East, savored the vision of a world ending in absolute oblivion, Heredia admired energy and achievement, and his fundamental concern was how to escape from oblivion. Like Leconte de Lisle he preferred the past to his own century; however, his preference did not manifest itself in savage hatred but in a certain aristocratic aloofness and a temperamental affinity with other ages. Like Leconte de Lisle he admired Greek antiquity, but with his zest for life, his curiosity about the unlimited possibilities of the mind, and especially with his profound admiration for art and beautiful objects, his mood was perhaps more akin to that of the Renaissance. It has been said of him, "He loves a brave man and a beautiful woman, a rich phrase and a fine cadence to it. What is splendid in colour, what is stately in movement, what is sonorous in sound, it is this which he chooses for himself and which he gives us."[7] These personal tastes explain in part his admiration for Greek civilization with its plastic beauty and heroism, for the Renaissance with its enthusiasm, energy and distinction in the arts, and for the tropics and the Orient with their color and exotic natural beauty.

I think we should guard against forming a picture of Heredia as a mere dilettante or an eclectic. Although personal tastes and temperament must have had something to do with what aspects of the past he emphasizes, the work derives its unity from other sources. Its dominant note, according to Heredia's famous contemporary Verlaine, is heroism, whether it be mythological, Castillian or esthetic.[8] The figures which people *Les Trophées* are largely heroic ones. They include gods and demi-gods, Japanese feudal warriors, Roman emperors, Hannibal the military strategist, Spanish *conquistadores*, Ladas the runner, the Lybian charioteer, and, perhaps most important of all, artists and craftsmen. René Doumic has gone so far as to say that for Heredia the only moments that are significant in history are the heroic ones.[9] It is difficult to disagree with such a statement if we broaden the meaning of "heroic" to include the idea of beauty. Beauty and heroism are scarcely separable for Heredia; the artist-hero, maker of beautiful things, is everywhere present, from the unnamed architects of the ruined temple in the opening sonnet to the also unnamed sculptor in the closing sonnet. Between the two we find an abundance of artists and craftsmen, writers, carpenters, smiths, sculptors, engravers, enamelers, painters and book binders. Those heroes who do not create beautiful objects leave behind by the greatness of their deeds some vestige of the beauty of life. Life by its very definition means beauty for Heredia, and a hero is someone who has not passed through life without leaving some trace of himself behind as an affirmation of the existence of man.

In this connection we cannot, however, speak of *Les Trophées* as some kind of representation of humanity's spiritual evolution. Whereas Hugo envisages man as rising and Leconte de Lisle is convinced that the quality of human life has degenerated with the advent of Christianity, Heredia upholds no thesis about either the progress or regression of man. He is more concerned with presenting the various manifestations of beauty through the ages. Although history has clothed man differently and changed his decor, he has, through the ages, remained the same at the most basic level. The common denominator is his mortality. Man is a creature who is alive to the beauty of existence, is aware that death comes soon, sees that by contrast with his own condition nature is immutable, and seeks immortality through creeds, heroic action, creative activity, anything in fact which will save him from oblivion.

IV   An Elegiac Undertone

Les Trophées are almost like one large poem devoted to this theme, and the sonnets themselves are in a real sense traces or vestiges suggesting the multi-faceted richness of the past, and thus of life. Despite the dominant heroic note, which is a trade mark of the epic, and despite the panoramic vistas of history which we sometimes glimpse, Heredia's view of man in Les Trophées is really lyric and elegiac. His main themes are those of the greatest lyric poetry. He is concerned with the joy of living and the reality of dying, and even as he evokes the beauty of life and man's dreams and heroic attempts to preserve himself from utter oblivion, he shows that these efforts are futile. Even monuments made from the hardest of materials are not durable enough to withstand the ravages of time. It is no accident that the opening and closing sonnets both present images of stone monuments in ruin. In these two sonnets and elsewhere, in "A un Triomphateur," for example, the contrast between the brevity and fragility of man's life and monuments and the permanence and strength of nature is conveyed by the image of grass and vines covering man's rocky ruins.

Despite the fact that Heredia sees greatness in high accomplishment and in facing death in a distinguished manner, his collection of sonnets is pervaded by the sentiment that human activity and agitation are futile. They are destined to end in silence and immobility like the Medieval lords and ladies in "Vitrail," who lie without voice, gesture or hearing, their rank, power and earthly accomplishments no longer of any consequence; or like the city of Carthagena in "A une Ville morte," drifting off to sleep beneath the eternal swaying of the palms, the flame of its glory extinguished for all time. And yet we notice that the lords and ladies, although sightless, continue to look, and that Carthagena is only sleeping. By placing such vestiges of life in his images of death Heredia conveys something of the strength of man's compelling attachment to life and his reluctance to let go of it.

Not only are these among the principal themes of lyric poetry, but the elegiac mood of *Les Trophées* is also evident in an underlying melancholy pervading the collection. Heredia is never angry, indignant or sentimental, nor does he resort to open complaints or self-pity. In art as in life his taste was impeccable. Emotion has been elevated and purified, leaving an impression of calm serenity. The color, sonorities, splendor and noble dignity of these sonnets tend to conceal the sadness which is at their core, as the limpid beauty of Racine's verse makes the reader forget the savage violence of the emotions of some of his greatest dramatic characters. Nonetheless, Heredia consistently communicates a sense of loss at the passing of life and beauty. He evokes with exquisite tenderness the sadness of those who experience such loss, whether it be the child crying over the grave of a dead insect or the young bride condemned to inexorable and dark Erebus at the moment when life should have been at its richest and happiest. Unwilling to indulge in self-pity, he nevertheless sometimes invokes pity for those who suffer, as when he calls on the land and the sea to be gentle and silent toward the shipwrecked victim in "Le Naufragé." The sleeping city of Syracuse, calmly beautiful under a Mediterranean sky, conveys a touching but serene sadness at the thought that the beauty of the Sicilian maidens was so ephemeral. And the monuments fallen into ruin or overgrown with vegetation are themselves images of the passing of beauty and communicate the sadness of impermanence. Heredia bears no grudge against nature for not sharing man's fragile destiny. Nature for its part is not indifferent to man's fate. At least some measure of tender melancholy comes from an impression of sympathy, though usually not articulate, between nature and man. Life as Heredia presents it is almost never mediocre. If such were the case its passing might seem less sad. But when life has been rich, distinguished, intense and beautiful, as it is in *Les Trophées*, the very fact that it must end leaves a stamp of restrained sadness everywhere.

Beneath Heredia's historical erudition and epic framework we thus find a discreet elegiac poet, a fact which did not go unnoticed by some of his contemporaries, as the following lines from the pen of his friend François Coppée will show:

Nous savons le coin où se réfugie,
Sous les fleurs de pourpre et d'or enfoui,
Le discret parfum de ton élégie.[10]

We know the spot where, buried beneath the flowers of purple and gold, the
discreet perfume of your elegy takes refuge.

have no historical connection have an exotic flavor lending an impression of distance, which makes them compatible with a feeling of the past. In this sense "Sieste" and "Fleur séculaire" are thus suitably placed. "La Nature et le Rêve," not closely tied to historical events, can be regarded as the logical conclusion of a historical sequence in that its perspective, besides often being timeless, is also contemporary, and in this way it may be integrated into the chronological plan of the collection after all.

II   *Sonnet Cycles*

When we come to the question of arrangement within the five sections, we discover Heredia's fondness for putting related sonnets into small groups, especially groups of two or three. Examples can be found in almost every section. In "La Grèce et la Sicile," for instance, "Ariane" and "Bacchanale" are both dominated by the figure of the god Bacchus. The first one evokes the intoxicated pleasure of Ariadne in anticipation of the kiss she will receive from Bacchus, who is making a triumphal appearance. The second presents a scene of wild orgy and offers a larger perspective than the first. Apart from the presence of Bacchus, the two poems have other common elements: tigers, grapes, intoxication, and loud sounds. In most of these groups or cycles the main common bond is a person or persons. "La Trebbia" and "Après Cannes" recall the Punic Wars and both are dominated by an atmosphere of lurking terror inspired by Hannibal. "Epiphanie" and "Le Huchier de Nazareth" are grouped together because the central figure in each is Christ.

Among the groups of three we find one devoted to Perseus and Andromeda, one to Antony and Cleopatra, one to Heredia's ancestor Don Pedro, and still another to the Egyptian Khèm. The grouping into three seems to be particularly useful in presenting a narrative which is too long for a single sonnet, in marking three successive stages or aspects of an action or scene, and in providing three different perspectives or points of view. As an illustration we can take the trilogy devoted to Perseus and Andromeda. In it we find not only too much material for one sonnet, but also three successive stages of an action. First, in "Andromède au monstre" Perseus, mounted on Pegasus, descends to free the chained Andromeda. Then, in "Persée et Andromède," having placed Andromeda on Pegasus, Perseus himself mounts and they rise into the air. The third stage of the action, found in "Le Ravissement d'Andromède," is their cosmic flight into starry space. The trilogy devoted to Antony and Cleopatra is comparable to a triptych, each part giving a different perspective of the same subject. "Le Cydnus" focuses on Cleopatra, exotic, beautiful and dangerous, like a bird of prey. "Soir de Bataille" evokes the proud figure of Antony, wounded and bleeding but nonetheless courageous and masterful. The third sonnet brings the two persons together, both dominating in their own way, and suggests the triumph of the more subtle power of Cleopatra over the more forthright strength of Antony, foreshadowing the decline of Antony's fortunes and those of the empire.

We also find a certain number of pairings in which the sonnets belong to different sections and thus cannot be placed adjacent to each other. We can think of them as parallel or corresponding sonnets, repetitions with variations which are like echoes of each other and thus knit together and help to unite the collection as a whole. In "L'Exilée" the exiled Sabinula nostalgically reminiscing about her childhood spent in Rome recalls "L'Esclave," where the slave longs for the beauty of his Sicilian home and for his beloved Clearista. The carnage involving the Roman legions in "Soir de Bataille" echoes the battle scene of the Greek poem "Le Thermodon," depicting the river's banks strewn with bodies of the dead, while its waters carry away more dead together with weapons and chariots. In both the Greek "Le Chevrier" and the Roman "La Flûte" a herdsman is invited to forget his animals and enjoy the pleasure and abandon of music. In the Renaissance poem "A une Ville morte" the image of the sleeping city Carthagena looks ahead to a similar one of Syracuse in "La Nature et le Rêve." "Les Funérailles" from the same section evokes the mountains of Greece and makes us think of the panoramic Greek landscape in "Sur l'Othrys," the last poem of the Greek and Sicilian section. "Vendange" in "La Nature et le Rêve" reminds us that the grapes still grow under the same skies as in ancient days, but in the modern landscape Bacchus is missing. The Greek equivalent of this grape harvest is the Bacchanalian festivities evoked in "Bacchanale." As a last example we may consider "Le Récif de corail" from "L'Orient et les Tropiques" and "La Sieste" from "La Nature et le Rêve." Both are like paintings presenting shifting patterns of light and color, the former in a tropical ocean setting, the latter in a drowsy and hot noon landscape.

In addition to his arrangements in two's and three's, Heredia sometimes assembles sonnets in larger cycles. Thus, six poems are devoted to Hercules and the centaurs, five to Artemis and the nymphs, four to the Roman household gods under the title "Hortorum Deus," and eight to the Spanish *conquistadores.*

III   Key Poems

Within the five sections it seems to me we can find a number of key poems comparable to pillars or girders reinforcing the structure of the whole. In some ways they, more than other sonnets, condense the sense of *Les Trophées.* Most frequently placed at the beginning or at the end of a section, but sometimes in the other parts of it, they serve to introduce, conclude and reinforce.

The first of these key poems is "L'Oubli." It opens not only the Greek and Sicilian section but the whole of *Les Trophées.* Its title is significant, for *l'oubli,* or oblivion, is precisely the enemy to whom Heredia addresses himself in the collection. Ephemeral man, whose monuments do not endure, is in the presence of immutable nature. The ruined temple at the summit of the promontory is sufficiently Greek to allow "L'Oubli" to take its place among the Greek sonnets. The section ends with "Sur l'Othrys." In it we contemplate the Greek world from an elevated physical perspective and in the manner of a film fade-out we see before us one last panoramic view of the terrain we have just explored in greater detail, before passing on to another civilization. Nearly at the mid-point of the Greek and Sicilian poems Heredia has placed "Le Vase" to function somewhat like a central pillar supporting the structures on either side. The vase in question has on it engravings of scenes and subjects from sonnets preceding this one as well as from some which follow it. In this way it knits together many of the fabrics which compose the Greek and Sicilian cycle. Among these scenes we find first of all Jason and Medea with the fleece in the forest of Colchis, recalling the sonnet "Jason et Medée." Then we see the intoxicated Bacchae, whom we shall find again in "Bacchanale." The battle scene showing horsemen clashing and dead heroes being brought back on their shields echoes parts of "Le Thermodon," while the plaintive old men and mothers grieving for their sons prepare us for such poems as "Epigramme votive" and "La Prière du mort." The last picture on the vase is that of the chimera which we meet again several sonnets later in "Sphinx."

"Rome et les Barbares" opens with "Pour le Vaisseau de Virgile." While this sonnet cannot be regarded as central to the thought of *Les Trophées,* it is important structurally in that it forms the transition between the Greek and the Roman poems. It does so symbolically through Virgil's voyage to the Greek islands of the Cyclades, thus representing the Latin world making contact with the Greek world. "L'Exilée" forms a fitting conclusion to the Roman and Barbarian section in a way which recalls "Sur l'Othrys." Both offer a last look at the civilization just presented; however, in "L'Exilée" the view of Rome is not a physical perception but an image which exists in the memory of the exiled woman. A key poem in terms of the meaning of Les Trophées is "A un Triomphateur." It is to the Roman section what "L'Oubli" is to the Greek. The marble sculpture destined to preserve the memory of Roman glory yields to the more durable grass by which it is overgrown. This poem contains a verse which appears to be a rather pessimistic commentary on the title and spirit of the whole collection: "Un vil lierre suffit à disjoindre un trophée" (A lowly vine is all it takes to split a trophy). Perhaps in placing this sonnet between those evoking Hannibal's victories and the trilogy of Antony and Cleopatra, Heredia was making an appropriate commentary on the fragility of even Rome's greatness.

Although "Le Moyen Age et la Renaissance" contains few poems inspired by the Middle Ages, the opening poem "Vitrail" in large measure compensates for this paucity. By itself it evokes much of what we associate with that period and conveys a vivid sense of its cathedrals with their stained-glass windows, its Crusades, its feudal organization, and the lives of its lords and ladies. "Les Conquérants" is another key poem in this division. It is the first of the sonnets devoted to the Spanish conquerors and is thus suitably situated between them and the other Renaissance poems. Besides capturing the Renaissance spirit of adventure and men's desire to expand their horizons, it resurrects the atmosphere of that period in Spanish history when the conquerors set forth to explore and colonize parts of the Western Hemisphere for Spain. It is a kind of prologue preceding the sonnets presenting more specific accomplishments of the conquistadores. But their efforts are futile too. That is the import of the closing sonnet of the section, "A une Ville morte." Carthagena, jewel of the Indies, crowning achievement of the conquerors, is in ruins, while the palm trees, as a part of immutable nature, endure forever.

In "L'Orient et les Tropiques" we might regard "Fleurs de feu" as another key poem. Its reference to the volcanic Chimborazos and a certain exotic distance justify its inclusion in this section, but it is a key poem for the collection as a whole more than for "L'Orient et les Tropiques." At first glance "Fleurs de feu" recalls such poems as

"L'Oubli" and "A un Triomphateur"; in all three vegetable life in some way triumphs over, disintegrates, obscures or outlives rock. But in "Fleurs de feu" the rock is a volcano, not a man-made monument. It has existed from time immemorial and has its own eternity. Yet a lowly cactus flower bursts through the rock, grows, blooms, and spreads its pollen. The living organism cannot be repressed by the inanimate rock. In its own way it is more powerful than the volcano. The last three verses of the sonnet suggest that the emergence and flowering of the cactus can be compared to a volcanic eruption. It is this strong affirmation of the principle of life, irrepressible and ever renewed, which gives the sonnet its special significance within *Les Trophées*.

Heredia's last word in the collection is "vivant" (living), and it appears in the closing sonnet "Sur un marbre brisé." The latter is as effective in concluding *Les Trophées* as "L'Oubli" is in opening the book. Here we find another marble monument in ruins, overgrown with vines. The features of the statue are not recognizable, and the era of the god whose likeness it is lies far in the past. The main themes of the book are recapitulated: man's monuments have not endured, even the gods are not immortal, and only nature is permanent. The oblique rays convey the impression of the setting of the sun. Images of finality — the ruin of the statue, the end of the day, the end of an era — fittingly close the collection. But the breeze blows aside the vines covering the face of the statue, and in the dying sunlight, the god momentarily appears alive before darkness and the vines will again conceal it. Thus, just before we close Heredia's volume, his affirmation of life and regret for its loss are communicated to us one last time.

IV *Linking Techniques*

It is probable that many of the groupings I have pointed out are fairly obvious even after a first or second reading. Other bonds are more subtle and not so quickly discernable. The whole body of sonnets is remarkably well tied together, and it is rare to find a sonnet without some link to an adjacent one. I think this can be regarded as an indication of the skill with which Heredia arranged his sonnets and of his perceptiveness in discovering already existing elements in them to serve as linking agents.

One of these is what we might call an association of ideas. In this category we could include those sonnets containing some aspect of a subject — theme, situation, landscape, event or action — which suggests a similar one in an adjacent poem. For example, in the Greek section "Sphinx" follows "La Magicienne." The sorceress of the latter poem suggests the sphinx in that both embody the tyranny of irresistible desire and of destructiveness. "La Prière du mort" and "L'Esclave" are linked by a similarity of situation. In both an unfortunate person sends a message to a loved one; the first one ends with an evocation of a weeping mother, while the end of the second one refers to the sadness of the slave's solitary beloved. In "L'Orient et les Tropiques" the picture of the eruption of the volcanic Chimborazos sets up a series of associations. The image of the eruption, used a second time in "Fleurs de feu" to represent the bursting forth of the cactus flower, is repeated in the following poem "Fleur séculaire." In "Récif de Corail," which comes next, the image occurs again in the explosion of color and fire caused by the sudden movement of the large fish in the depths of an exotic tropical sea.

Sometimes in a group of more than two sonnets linked together by associations we find a progression within the sequence. This occurs, for example, in a group of three sonnets found in "La Nature et le Rêve." Glory is the theme which links them. The first of the three is "La Mort de l'aigle." The symbolism of the eagle's Icarus-like flight and death is explained in the last three verses: there is glory in death when it occurs in the accomplishment of some distinguished action for a noble cause. In each of the following two sonnets the spatial perspective is enlarged. The eagle rises only above the snowy mountain summits; in "Plus Ultra" the speaker experiences a compelling urge to seek glory by exploring hitherto unknown polar regions. "La Vie des Morts" concludes the spatial expansion by evoking the extraterrestrial region of stars through which the exalted souls of two poet friends rise, leaving behind the glory which makes them immortal.

Another linking effect is produced by the parallelism of the tercets, usually the last ones, in some adjacent sonnets. This similarity can appear in the general content, as in "Artemis" and "La Chasse." The tercets in both these sonnets evoke the horror and bloodshed produced by Artemis' appearance in the forest. Sometimes not only the content but also the vocabulary are similar. As an illustration let us examine the last tercet of "A un Fondateur de ville":

> Et seule, à ton cimier brille, ô Conquistador,
> Héraldique témoin des splendeurs de ton rêve,
> Une ville d'argent qu'ombrage un palmier d'or.

And alone on your crest shines, oh conquistador, heraldic witness of your dream, a silver city shaded by a golden palm tree.

The last tercet of the next sonnet, "Au Même," is clearly similar:

> Aussi tes dernier fils, sans trèfle, ache ni perle,
> Timbrent-ils leur écu d'un palmier ombrageant
> De son panache d'or une Ville d'argent.

And so your last sons, without trefoil, apium or pearl, stamp their escutcheon with a palm tree shading a city of silver with its plume of gold.

The parallelism may also consist largely in the grammatical structure rather than in the content. In "La Nature et le Rêve," for example, the last tercet of "La Mort de l'aigle" echoes that of the preceding sonnet "Le Lit," although the two are not similar in content. Each of the tercets begins with the adjective "heureux," followed by a relative clause introduced by "qui." In addition, the second verse of each tercet begins with the preposition "dans."

A third way of connecting sonnets is through the repetition of words or phrases with or without minor changes, thus producing an echo effect. A fairly simple example is provided by "Le Cocher" and "Le Coureur," both from "La Grèce et la Sicile." Apart from the fact that both are concerned with racers, reason enough for placing them together, the phrase "Vers la palme et le but" (toward the palm and the goal) in the one is echoed in the other by "Vers le but et la palme." Often this repetition is limited to a single word, as in "La Chasse" and "Nymphée," both of which begin with "le quadrige" (the quadriga). But more complicated patterns of repetition can be found as well. In "Ariane" we can single out "grand tigre," "large rein," "rugissant," "noirs raisins" and "longs cris," while in "Bacchanale," the sonnet which follows, we find the corresponding expressions, "tigres," "reins rayés," "rugissant," "un noir raisin" and "les cris." Another variation on the technique of repetition is the echo effect of a key word in sonnets not placed together in the collection. For instance, in "Blason céleste" the word "vitrail" recalls the poem "Vitrail," the echo being reinforced through an allusion in both sonnets to Medieval crusades.

Probably Heredia's subtlest form of linking is achieved through repetition of rhymes and sonorities. As we might expect, this occurs most frequently in sonnets which are already related in some way.

Several degrees of sound repetition can be found, including complete identity of some of the rhyming words, identity of rhyme only, identity of the rhyming vowel only (assonance), and finally similarity of internal sound patterns. As a first example we may consider the two sonnets "Email" and "Rêves d'émail." All the rhymes of the sestet of "Email" are repeated in "Rêves d'émail," which immediately follows it. The rhyming words of the sestet in question are "saphir," "Ophir," "Penthésilée," "encor," "ailée" and "or." All of these are echoed in the rhyme words of the first ten verses of "Rêves d'émail": "athanor," "rougie," "magie," "or," "essor," "mythologie," "orgie," "chrysaor," "Penthésilée" and "exilée." It will be noted that two of the six ("Penthésilée" and "or") are repeated identically, two more ("saphir" and "Ophir") are echoed as assonances in "rougie," "magie," "mythologie" and "orgie," while the two remaining ones ("encor" and "ailée") rhyme with the words in "-or" and "-tée" respectively.

In some adjacent sonnets we find a similarity of rhymes and assonances not only between the tercets of the first and the quatrains of the second, but also between the quatrains of the first and the tercets of the second. The result is a rather pleasing symmetry which makes us think of the effect of a chiasmus. Thus, if we write down the last word of each verse of "Soir de Bataille" and "Antoine et Cléopâtre," we can readily see the X-shaped pattern of the correspondence of sounds:

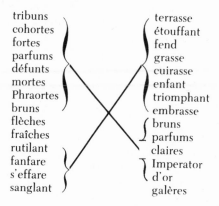

In addition we notice that "flèches" and "fraîches" are in assonance with "claires" and "galères," all four of these situated in the tercets.

As a final example, let us consider "Ariane" and "Bacchanale." Here we see, in addition to repetition of rhymes and assonances, an outstanding illustration of similar internal sound patterns. In the first tercet of "Ariane" we find the following verse:

Parmi *les noirs raisins rouler ses* grappes d'*ambre.

This is echoed by a verse in the second quatrain of "Bacchanale":

Rougit d'un *noir raisin les* gorges *et les* flancs.

If we now compare the sounds represented by the italicized letters we can readily see the close correspondence and even near identity of the sounds. Thus the pattern [i] [le] [nwar] [rezɛ̃] [ru] [le] [e] [g] [ã] is answered by [ru] [i] [nwar] [rezɛ̃] [le] [g] [e] [le] [ã].

V *Why the Sonnet Form*

When we turn away from the problem of the arrangement of the individual parts of *Les Trophées* to consider Heredia's art within the sonnet, the first question to be answered is, "Why did he choose this form?" In order to attempt an answer let us first glance briefly at the background of the sonnet in France.[2] It was probably introduced into French literature by Clément Marot and Mellin de Saint-Gelais at the beginning of the French Renaissance and was in high favor with some of the sixteenth-century poets, notably Ronsard and du Bellay, who almost at once became masters of the form. The word "sonnet" was derived from a word meaning song or poem. Old French contained the word "sonet," a diminutive of "son," which meant a song of love.[3] It is not surprising then that the French Renaissance sonnet was often intended to be sung, and was lyrical in character. It has been maintained by Heredia's son-in-law René Doumic that a basic element in the definition of the sonnet is its lyricism.[4] The high points in its history in France coincide with the sixteenth and nineteenth centuries, both notable for their lyric poetry. In the seventeenth century it was sometimes used as a kind of salon pastime, for example, in the Hôtel de Rambouillet. But it declined sharply and in the eighteenth century it had largely fallen into disuse.

One might have expected to find a revival of the sonnet with the advent of Romantic poetry, but such is not the case. Lamartine did not publish a single sonnet, while in the works of Vigny and Hugo together we can find no more than a handful, and these appeared toward the end of their lives when Romanticism, historically speaking, had passed. It was used more by minor Romantics than by the major ones, and it was chiefly Sainte-Beuve who can be credited with restoring it around 1830. Although the subjectivity which we usually associate with the Romantics should have been well suited to the lyrical nature of the sonnet, the major Romantics, not forgetting that one of the issues for which they had fought was freedom from rules, were unwilling to submit themselves to the constraints of a prescribed form. Perhaps also their tendency to communicate experience if possible in all its diversity and totality was incompatible with a form which appeared to permit little elaboration. A further point which seems worth mentioning is that apart from purely lyrical poetry, the Romantics had ambitious aspirations to write historical and epic poetry, and the vast perspectives required for this seemed irreconcilable with the sonnet form.

With the younger Romantics and their successors we notice a reaction against the lack of restraint in the poetic style of their predecessors. This reaction, with its emphasis on craftsmanship, moderation and perfection of form, finds a perfect vehicle in the sonnet. We observe that not only Sainte-Beuve but also Gautier and Baudelaire as well as many of the Parnassian poets, including Heredia of course, employed it.

Heredia's position, however, is special, for he used the sonnet almost to the exclusion of all other verse forms. The foregoing remarks help us to see in part why he might have done so. But I think we must consider other factors as well. In a letter of 1896 to Edmund Gosse, Heredia writes as follows:

> Si je m'en suis tenu au sonnet, c'est que je trouve que dans sa forme mystique et mathématique [. . .] il exige, par sa brièveté et sa difficulté, une conscience dans l'exécution et une concentration de la pensée qui ne peuvent qu'exciter et pousser à la perfection l'artiste digne de ce beau nom.[5]

> If I have kept to the sonnet it is because I find that in its mystical and mathematical form [. . .] it demands through its brevity and difficulty an awareness in its execution and a concentration of thought which cannot but rouse and spur on to perfection an artist worthy of that fine name.

In his address at the unveiling of du Bellay's statue at Ancenis in September, 1894, Heredia had called the sonnet the most perfect of fixed-form poems, adding that it requires very sure taste and unusual mastery on the part of the poet, particularly in the choice of words in which the idea and the difficult and important rhymes will be concentrated. Apart from responding to the artistic creed which Heredia shared with other Parnassians, the sonnet must have appeared to him in some ways a form particularly compatible with some aspects of his temperament. In the preface to his *Rimes héroïques* of 1843, Auguste Barbier had observed that the sonnet was capable of rising to the proudest notes and of expressing the most masculine accents.[6] Heredia saw that it was not suited to the banal, the mediocre or the platitudinous, but that he could use it instead as a vehicle for what was elevated, vigorous and distinguished. In short, it suited his aristocratic as well as artistic temperament.

There were also important points of incompatibility between him and the sonnet form. Ironically, these may have drawn him to the sonnet as much as the affinities of temperament did. It is well to recall at this point that in his daily life and social relationships Heredia tended to be exuberant, lively, enthusiastic and spontaneous. He liked to be in the forefront of conversations, was sometimes impetuous and had a penchant for expressing himself in superlatives. Even in his earliest verse we may find some of these characteristics. However, he seems to have been attracted early to the sonnet as a form which would counteract the excesses in his temperament and curb the spontaneous current of feeling through the discipline and concentration required. In any event, he shared with a number of France's first-rate writers the notion of the difficulty of artistic form, and in some ways looked ahead to Valéry's conception. The stringent rules of the sonnet were welcomed by him; they were not obstacles so much as paths leading to high artistic accomplishment. It was in the perfection of form, toward which the sonnet forced Heredia to strive, that he saw the best chance for the survival of his work, and in this sense his choice of form becomes an integral part of that organic whole whose purpose is to defeat or at least combat oblivion. His daughter, in a rather ingenious comparison between him and his ancestors, who built walls around cities, calls her father the "seigneur des sonnets infranchissables" (the lord of impassable sonnets) and suggests that the sonnets, like walls, enclose what he has created so as to protect it and make it last.[7]

VI *The Last Verse*

It is no exaggeration to suggest that with Heredia the sonnet attained one of the highest points in its history. Such a judgment need not be limited to the sonnet in France; in other countries as well Heredia came to be regarded as one of the most outstanding sonneteers. In the *Fortnightly Review* near the beginning of this century, for example, we find the following evaluation of his importance: "Consciously or unconsciously, the type of sonnet elaborated by Heredia has for the last twelve years at least been that which the great variety of sonneteers has, the world over, with every variety of equipment, with greater or less success, endeavoured to reproduce."[8]

Few would dispute the claim that his craftsmanship and his respect for the rules of the sonnet were impeccable. But his main contributions reach further. We have seen that the sonnet was for the most part a lyrical form. It often bore traces of Petrarch and tended to be subjective, the most confidential of poetic species, according to Edmund Gosse.[9] But in Heredia's hands it became something more. He gave it a new versatility, so that within the limitations of its form it acquired a certain air of objectivity and was capable of rendering a much greater variety of tones, idyllic, dramatic, narrative and epic, to the extent that these are possible in a lyric genre. However, I think Heredia's greatest achievement is that in a remarkably large number of his sonnets he has been able to make a fourteen-verse poem communicate a richness of content and meaning which we should normally expect to find only in a longer poem. This implies mastery of the technique of compression. In so far as both Hugo and Heredia attempted to present frescoes of humanity through the ages, the technique of the two poets differs markedly. Whereas Hugo constructs vast panels of history, Heredia gives us condensations of such scenes. Just as his trophies are traces of the endless richness of life, so the scant fourteen verses of a sonnet are suggestions of vast perspectives toward which they point. In this way his technique of compression is an organic part of the central significance of his book.

In a sense his technique is telescopic in character: he gives the reader a small aperture to look through but in the distance wide horizons and panoramic vistas open up. The effect for which he strove corresponds to that which he admired in Daniel Vierge's art, which gave "dans un dessin de quelques centimètres, l'illusion de la foule innombrable et grouillante des architectures démesurées, des immenses espaces, des perspectives infinies"[10] (within a drawing of a few centimeters, the illusion of swarming, innumerable masses, of measureless architecture, of immense spaces, of infinite perspectives). Many of his sonnets are like compression chambers whose full contents are released, sometimes with explosive force, at the end. Thus it is usually the last verse which can be compared to the large magnifying lens of a telescope or to the release valve of the compressor, and it is perhaps the last verse which constitutes Heredia's most significant innovation. It was customary for the last verse of a sonnet to close the thought of the poem much as a period indicates the end of a sentence and causes the reader's voice to fall. "Chute" (fall) is the French word commonly used to designate this last verse. It was generally accepted too that it should be a striking verse so as to close the poem with a definitive ring. Heredia, however, rarely follows this practice. Instead of "sealing" the sonnet, so to speak, his last verse opens it and allows its contents to take flight. Instead of a "chute" it is normally an "envol" (flight).

Not all of his last verses take flight in a narrow meaning of the word, but most of them do open an expanded perspective. It is rare to find in *Les Trophées* an undistinguished last verse, such as the rather prosaic one which closes "Le Lit" by referring to the paternal bed as follows: "Où tous les siens sont nés aussi bien qu'ils sont morts" (Where all his family were born and also died). As a rule Heredia demonstrates remarkable skill, perhaps even virtuosity, in the variety of effects he produces in these expanded final impressions. It would be difficult to appreciate fully this variety without considering most of the sonnets individually, but I shall try to give some notion of it by dealing with those effects and techniques which appear to me to stand out most.

One of these is enlargement through a shadow or silhouette effect, comparable to the lengthening of shadows in the evening. While this enlargement is of course physical, it also suggests a non-material component. For example, in "Fuite des Centaures" the centaurs see lengthening behind them in the moonlight "La gigantesque horreur de l'ombre Herculéenne" (The gigantic horror of the Herculean shadow). This last verse not only enlarges the shadow but also the stature of the pursuing Hercules, and above all suggests the enormous terror which he inspires in the centaurs. "Soir de Bataille" offers a good example of a silhouette. The last verse, which evokes the bleeding emperor silhouetted against the flaming sky, not only enlarges him in stature physically and as a heroic figure, but also lends an epic perspective through the suggestive image of the sky.

Another type of enlargement is produced by images suggesting limitlessness in time and space. In "Armor" the sight of the ocean merging with the darkness of the evening to obscure the horizon conveys a feeling of "l'ivresse de l'espace et du vent intrépide" (the intoxication of space and intrepid wind). In "L'Oubli" the last verse, suggesting both the immensity and the eternity of the ocean, is especially effective as a contrast to the transience and fragility of man's destiny presented earlier in the sonnet. A remarkable image of timelessness is the one given by the last verse of "Vitrail," a verse which, it is said, took Heredia ten years to find. Once again man's mortality is opposed to nature's eternity. The verse in question is "La rose du vitrail toujours épanouie" (The eternally blooming rose of the stained-glass window). It may seem strange that Heredia has chosen the most delicate, fragile and short-lived of flowers to form part of an image of immutability. Yet it makes us think of the fragility of life itself and of man's wish that life, however delicate, might endure. It echoes the preceding verse, which evokes the sightless stone eyes staring at the window. The two verses oppose one another, immobilize one another, and complete an image of frozen life so typical of Heredia's vision, in which the affirmation of life with all its vital energy seems almost strong enough to produce a stalemate of immobility in the face of inexorable death.

A characteristic common to many of Heredia's last verses is that they suggest or contain some notion of elevation. This can of course occur as flight in its narrow sense. Thus in "La Flûte" the herdsman is invited to learn the divine art of flute playing so that his sighs of love, transformed by the sacred instrument, may fly upward mingled with harmonious breath. In a significantly large number of poems the idea of elevation connected with the last verse manifests itself in some type of upward movement from earth to heaven or the stars. In the second sonnet of the Perseus and Andromeda cycle Pegasus, responding to his master's command, rises with a gigantic bound from the ocean and "bat le ciel ébloui de ses ailes de flamme" (beats the dazzled sky with his wings of flame). In the third sonnet Perseus and Andromeda have flown high into the heavens and see their celestial constellation. In "Mer montante" the last verse evokes the rather pessimistic idea that man and the sea, those two great abysses according to Victor Hugo's "Ce qu'on entend sur la montagne," both eternally direct their voices heavenward seeking communication with the divine, but to no avail.

The notion of elevation or flight does not necessarily suggest aspiration toward God, but some idea of ennoblement or of striving

toward some loftier attainment or conception of man is usually present. It can take the form of a transition from the material to the
spiritual plane, as in "Vélin doré," where the delicate vellum of a
volume bound and gilded by a master craftsman and long ago
touched by beautiful ladies recalls through some mysterious charm
"l'âme de leur parfum et l'ombre de leur rêve" (the soul of their perfume and the shadow of their dream). The transition can also be
from the literal to the figurative: in "Les Conquérants," for example, the explorers having reached an unfamiliar part of the world see
new stars rising from the depths of the ocean. In as much as they see
stars which were not visible from their homeland, the last verse can
be accepted literally as a description of the reflection they see in the
ocean; but figuratively, the new stars may suggest new experiences,
the excitement of the unknown, the possibility of "epic tomorrows"
already referred to in the sonnet. Still another form of flight is
through a transformation akin to apotheosis, such as we find in "Le
Cocher." The speed of this charioteer is so great that his chariot
seems ablaze with fire (which incidentally suggests Apollo's chariot
of the sun), and its movement gives the illusion of flight upward.
    Many examples could be cited of last verses which create a
richness of suggestive or dream quality through some unexpected
detail or image. Such a vision comes to mind in "A une Ville morte,"
where the unforgettable image of the "long frémissement
des palmes" is like an enchantment, holding the dead city under a
spell of timeless sleep. Or perhaps we might choose "Soleil
couchant," in which near the end the almost Baudelairean sunset,
with the sun dying against a rich and somber sky, undergoes a
sudden and magic transformation in the last verse, as the sun "closes
the golden boughs of its red fan," replacing the heaviness of gloom
with the light and airy charm of the world of fancy. The unexpected
can also occur as a sudden reversal. "Marsyas" is a good example.
This satyr, so accomplished as a player upon the reeds that he was
the master of animals and birds, has been silenced by the vengeance
of Apollo, and from a player upon an object of nature he has become
a plaything of nature, for the wind now plays upon his hide attached
to a yew tree. Another way in which the last verse sometimes sur-
prises is by arresting the action, preferably at its climax, thus leaving
its possible outcome to the imagination of the reader. In "Pan," for
example, the last verse is as follows: "Disparaît . . . Et les bois retom-
bent au silence" (Disappears . . . And the woods fall back into

silence again). "Disparaît" suspends the action at the moment when
Pan has just seized an unsuspecting nymph and has disappeared into
the woods with her. We are left to imagine the rest.

One of the best known of Heredia's sonnets, "Antoine et
Cléopâtre," exemplifies still another type of last verse, one which ex-
pands into a prophetic vision. It may be recalled that in this sonnet
Antony is holding Cleopatra in an ardent embrace. As he bends over
her, gazing into her eyes, the latter are transformed into an immense
ocean, and the specks of light in them become fleeing galleys. The
last verse can thus be taken to constitute a foreshadowing of the
flight of Cleopatra's vessels as they abandoned Antony's fleet of
galleys at the Battle of Actium.

VII   *Mirroring*

Another striking feature of Heredia's sonnets is a technique which
has been called mirroring. A. R. Chisholm explains it thus: "I
realized that Heredia's finesse took the form of half-concealed images or suggestions . . . as I was rereading 'Après Cannes,' I suddenly
realized that his inner form consisted partly of mirroring·effects —
very much like the 'correspondences' cultivated by the Symbolists."[11] In an earlier article Chisholm offers a more precise definition when he states that through the mirror technique "Heredia sees
an event, a thought, a view, reflected by another event, thought or
view as by the image of an object in a mirror."[12]

In so far as the inner human world is reflected by some aspect of
the material world, or one order of perception by another, this
mirroring is indeed very much like the Symbolist conception of correspondences. This is not the only kind of mirroring, however.
Sometimes we find a confrontation of images from the same order of
existence. At other times what we find is not a visual reflection at all
but an echo. In any event, two facts stand out concerning this
technique. The first is that it can be found in nearly all of the sonnets
in *Les Trophées*. The second is that the term "mirroring" appears
particularly apt because in so many instances where this reflection
occurs we find some kind of reversal of the image, just as a mirror
reverses an image. As a simple example we may take the sonnet
"Epiphanie." The first verse, "Donc, Balthazar, Melchior et Gaspar,
les Rois Mages," is reflected by the last verse, "Les Rois Mages
Gaspar, Melchior et Balthazar." It is obvious that the latter is almost
a complete reversal of the order of the words from the first verse. We
may think of such a construction containing some type of

symmetrical inversion as a form of chiasmus. In "Centaures et Lapithes" the last verse echoes the first more subtly through a repetition of the vowel sounds [u] and [y]. The two examples just cited are based on verbal and vowel repetition and, although they are not isolated instances, this kind of mirroring is not the most typical in *Les Trophées*. The mirror reflections which occur most often do not depend principally on repetition of sounds or words but on a correspondence among ideas, emotions or images, sometimes easily discernable but often partly concealed and not evident at first reading. We may recall that in "Stymphale" Hercules destroys the man-eating birds, the Stymphalides. They are so numerous that they conceal the sun like a layer of clouds. As Hercules lets fly his arrows into this mass of birds, holes open in these black clouds until they are dispersed and reveal the sun regarding Hercules, who in turn smiles up at the blue sky. It is of course correct to see a comparison here: just as the sun dispels the clouds with its rays, so Hercules disperses the birds with his arrows. But the important point is that the two parts of the comparison stand in the same relationship to each other as an object and its mirror image, and the spatial symmetry of the object and its reflection is preserved. The reflecting plane is at the level of the clouds, so that the layer of birds and the clouds merge and become one. The assimilation of one to the other is suggested, not explicitly stated. Equidistant from this plane but on opposite sides are Hercules and the sun facing one another and sharing between them a certain quality of solar divinity.

Since mirroring can be found in most of Heredia's *Trophées*, and since, as already mentioned, Professor Chisholm has treated the subject fully, little can be gained by offering a large number of examples. I should like, however, to cite "Floridum Mare," as an illustration of a sonnet whose very structure is based on the mirror technique:

> La moisson débordant le plateau diapré
> Roule, ondule et déferle au vent frais qui la berce;
> Et le profil, au ciel lointain, de quelque herse
> Semble un bateau qui tangue et lève un noir beaupré.

> Et sous mes pieds, la mer, jusqu'au couchant pourpré,
> Céruléenne ou rose ou violette ou perse
> Ou blanche de moutons que le reflux disperse,
> Verdoie à l'infini comme un immense pré.

Aussi les goëlands qui suivent la marée,
Vers les blés murs que gonfle une houle dorée,
Avec des cris joyeux, volaient en tourbillons;

Tandis que, de la terre, une brise emmiellée
Eparpillait au gré de leur ivresse ailée
Sur l'Océan fleuri des vols de papillons.

The grain overflowing the speckled plateau rolls, undulates and unfurls in
the cool wind which rocks it; and the outline of a harrow against the distant
sky seems like a boat which pitches and raises a black bowsprit. And beneath
my feet, the sea, right up to the western horizon, crimson, azure or rose or
violet or sea-green or white with sheep which the ebb-tide disperses, is
endlessly green like an immense meadow. So the sea gulls, which follow the
tide, were flying with a swirling motion and with joyous cries toward the ripe
crops distended by a golden swell, while from the land a honey-laden breeze
was scattering, according to the whims of their winged rapture, flights of
butterflies over the flowering ocean.

We can see that this sonnet consists of a series of alternating reflections between the sea and the land. In the first quatrain the grain
field reflects the sea by its wavelike motion, while the distant
harrow, likened to a boat, completes the seascape. In the second
quatrain the sea, reflecting the land, is green like the meadows,
strewn with many colors like the flowers of the meadow, while the
foam of the waves gives the appearance of sheep scattered here and
there. The two tercets reproduce these reflections. The fields of ripe
grain are seen in terms of the ocean, which in turn is covered with
flowers. But the tercets are less static than the quatrains. The boundaries between land and sea tend to be blurred as each of these two
aspires to the state of the other. This aspiration is conveyed by the
sea gulls which with joyous cries fly toward the land, and by the
butterflies, creatures of the land, which are scattered over the ocean
by the breeze blowing out from the land. Thus an element of the sea
joins the landscape while an element of the land becomes part of the
seascape.

We may ask at this point what contribution mirroring makes to
Heredia's poetry. We have already seen that many of his mirror images are comparisons and therefore are related to simile, metaphor
and symbol, or create "correspondences" somewhat as the Symbolist
poets envisaged them. To that extent, then, Heredia's poetry gains a
richness of suggestive power from mirroring. But the technique

taken in a global sense, even when mirror images have no suggestive or figurative dimension, fulfills the important function of acting as a unifying force. Earlier in this chapter it was noted that key poems echoing one another either in the same section or in different ones serve such a purpose. They are, in fact, special cases of mirroring: as whole poems they correspond to one another, reflecting each other's ideas and images. Within individual sonnets mirroring helps to create the effect of a tightly knit structure. The most frequent mirror image, although by no means the only one, found within individual sonnets is that in which there is a correspondence between the first quatrain and the last tercet or between the second quatrain and the first tercet, again suggesting a chiasmus-like symmetry which conveys a particular sense of wholeness and unity.

VIII *Other Symbolist Techniques*

The double image, that is, the object and its reflection, achieved by mirroring provides a second look as it were, and thus the possibility of added clarity and precision. However, the two corresponding images are not complete duplicates of each other since, as we have seen, the last verse in many sonnets tends to make them open-ended. Heredia thus achieves a curious effect of precision, clarity and stability, while at the same time opening up an undelineated world of suggestion, dream and mystery.

Perhaps that is what the celebrated critic Jules Lemaître had in mind when he said that each of Heredia's sonnets resumes at the same time "beaucoup de science et beaucoup de rêve" (much knowledge and much dream).[13] His remark can scarcely fail to recall the well known "Art poétique" in which Verlaine judges that "nothing is more precious than the gray song where the imprecise and the precise unite." It can hardly be maintained that Heredia's sonnets are "gray songs." Nor do the imprecise and the precise fuse. But the fact is that both elements are there, and the former, as it is allied to suggestiveness and subtle evocation, makes us think of Symbolist techniques. It may well be that his poetry is among the most perfect embodiments of the Parnassian esthetic, but it is not only that. Consider for a moment the following verses:

> Mon âme est devenue une prison sonore:
> Et comme en tes replis pleure et soupire encore
> La plainte du refrain de l'ancienne clameur;

Ainsi du plus profond de ce coeur trop plein d'Elle,
Sourde, lente, insensible et pourtant éternelle,
Gronde en moi l'orageuse et lointaine rumeur.

My soul has become a sonorous prison, and as in your inner recesses still weeps and sighs the complaint of the refrain of the ancient outcry, so from the depths of my heart too much filled with it, muffled, slow, imperceptible and yet eternal, rumbles in me the stormy and distant uproar.

If we did not know that these lines came from Heredia's "La Conque," we might be tempted to attribute them to Baudelaire. The first verse presents a metaphor of a type commonly found in Symbolist poetry where the soul is identified with some element of the material world. This is followed by a simile, a form not much in favor with the Symbolists, but Heredia succeeds in giving it a suggestive power characteristic of much Symbolist poetry. Here it evokes the age-old mystery of the human condition and the secret harmonies existing among the soul, the heart, prison, the sea shell and the ocean, each of which prolongs and reinforces the resonance of the image.

It would be wrong to think that all Parnassian poetry is bathed in the burning light of a tropical sun, leaving objects in a naked and shadowless relief. In Heredia this would be the exception rather than the rule. We find on the contrary that he prefers sunset, evening and moonlight to either dawn or noon. The "soleil mourant, sur un ciel riche et sombre" (dying sun, against a rich and somber sky), for example, which we find in his "Soleil couchant," conveys something of the melancholy of a Baudelairean sunset. It is in this vague world of half-tones, of light mingled with shadow, that Heredia's poetry is often at its most suggestive, evoking, for example, the terror inspired by Hercules through the lengthening of his menacing shadow at twilight, the hallucinatory vision of an ancient Egyptian graveyard which appears to come to life, the dreams of an exile in the evening, the picture of an old land shrouded in timeless mystery, or the strange and brooding melancholy beauty of sunset itself.

Since the time of Edgar Alan Poe, much has been said about pure poetry. The Symbolists aspired toward this ideal, and the whole question of pure poetry has been hotly debated since then. More than one meaning has been attached to the term. It may designate a kind of purification through which personal emotion becomes transfigured and removed from the passions of ordinary life and is elevated to a serene sadness and an indefinable nostalgia. In this sense perhaps Racine's poetry could also be considered pure. In this connection Heredia's attempt to achieve objectivity is less a matter of scientific attitude than of poetic insight. The underlying and yet not directly stated melancholy which permeates *Les Trophées*, the restraint, the elevation and impression of aristocratic taste, are all attributes which would allow us to regard his poetry as pure in this first sense.

For many of the Symbolists the term came to mean absence of prosaic elements, such as statement, description, moralizing, and in fact anything which could be expressed in prose. Essentially this meant a conception of poetry whose esthetic effects approach those of music. It implied a subordination of the everyday or practical meanings of words to their phonetic qualities, "le son qui donne le sens" (sound which gives the sense), as Alain puts it. It further implied a freeing of versification and syntactic patterns in order to achieve greater fluidity and subtleness of rhythm, so as to produce something of the suggestive effects of music.

In this connection Heredia was no great innovator, and yet his own convictions and practice were often not so different from those of the Symbolists. He had great respect for words; that is, for their physical presence, their reality as objects and not merely transparent signs pointing to practical meanings. There are some parallels to be drawn between him and Mallarmé. They shared the conception of poetry as a difficult art; both attempted, by introducing an element of unusual or rare usage, to reduce or break long-standing, accepted patterns of meaning attached to language. But while Mallarmé readily accepted words in current usage and achieved novelty and different associative patterns through changes in syntax, Heredia often uses rare words, technical or erudite terms or proper names, creating a splendor which has been compared to that of sparkling gems.[14] In his most hermetic poems Mallarmé approaches the point of unintelligibility because he has gone too far in ridding language of accepted meanings. While Heredia's poetry is not nearly so hermetic, we might suspect that many of his sonnets were left unfinished simply because he was reaching the limits of the possibilities of verbal communication also.

Heredia was clearly aware of the musical possibilities of verse and maintained that a beautiful verse contains its own music. However, he did not subscribe to the practice of free verse. His *Trophées* are written exclusively in alexandrines, most of which appear fairly traditional, although not rigid, in their rhythmic patterns. He regarded the alexandrine as the most polymorphous of verses, lending itself to infinite rhythmic variations. Besides, he felt, a poet could achieve with the alexandrine the same effects as with free verse. He takes as an example the following fragment from André Chénier:

> "Mon âme vagabonde à travers le feuillage
> Frémira. . . .

My wandering soul will tremble through the foliage,

He states that a Symbolist might have written it as one verse. Thus, what might for the latter be a beautiful sixteen-syllable verse is in reality only an alexandrine with a three-syllable *rejet*.[15] This judgment can be seriously questioned, since it can be contended that Chénier's arrangement will produce a longer pause after "feuillage," syntax notwithstanding, than the grouping in a single verse.

As for Heredia's own alexandrines, although he respects their traditional form he does not hesitate to introduce greater flexibility when he needs it. For example; he takes liberties with the caesura, making it more mobile as the situation demands. It is not unusual for him to place a definite or an indefinite article at the sixth syllable, followed by its noun in the seventh. This of course results in displacing the caesura and lending greater flexibility to the rhythm. He compensates for this by ensuring a strong and rich rhyme at the end of the verse. The effect of this is that Heredia is weakening the smaller rhythmic groups within the verse, while stressing the larger rhythmic unit of the verse. This is essentially what the Symbolists were doing when they extended rhythmic groups still further in free verse. Enjambement is not infrequent in *Les Trophées*, as we might expect from his pronouncement reported above. But perhaps its frequency is not as significant as the boldness of some of it. The enjambement used by poets before the Symbolists tended to be rather timid, in that the link between the *rejet* and the preceding word was usually relatively weak. By contrast, Heredia occasionally, but not frequently, makes the separation between words that are unquestionably closely linked and form a normally inseparable group. In "La Vie des morts," for example, we find these verses:

> La Gloire nous fera vivre à jamais parmi
> Les Ombres que la Lyre a faites fraternelles.

Glory will make us live forever in the shades which the Lyre has made fraternal.

Here the preposition "parmi" is cut off from its complement, and we have an instance of the kind of enjambement that was truly innovative and disruptive of long established patterns. Such examples, though rare in *Les Trophées*, represent a very modern practice of creating poetic tensions by reducing the coincidence of syntactic and rhythmic groups.

Rhyme is of paramount importance for Heredia. In this connection he took a much stronger stand than most of his Symbolist contemporaries, many of whom reacted not only against the use of rich rhymes but also against other time-honored practices in rhyming. According to some statistics, 61.2 percent of Heredia's rhymes in *Les Trophées* are rich, thus placing him third in rank behind Hugo and Banville.[16] If Heredia is a scrupulous craftsman, he avoids rigidity. Although manuscripts of his unfinished sonnets show that he usually began his poems by finding his rhymes, he does not sacrifice the propriety of words to them. On the contrary, they almost always suit the subject and are often key words in the total sense of a poem. As an illustration we may take the rhyming words of the second quatrain of "A un Fondateur de Ville." They are "périssable," "cimenté," "cité" and "sable." When we consider that the theme revolves about man's aspirations toward permanence on the one hand and the bitter reality that his condition is fragile and ephemeral on the other, we can readily see how aptly "cimenté" and "cité" suggest the durability which he seeks and how "périssable" and "sable" convey the idea of his precarious destiny.

Far from being an obstacle for Heredia, rhyme was rather a spur, even a springboard for him. By giving a high priority to it he was able to exercise a large degree of control in the elaboration of his sonnets, a control all the more necessary for a man normally given to enthusiasm and exuberance. He regarded rhyme as a means of creating that mysterious and suggestive state which the Symbolists admired in music. In a fragment of an unfinished poem entitled "A un poète" Heredia writes:

> Et la rime parfois prête au sens qu'elle achève
> Par l'éclat, la douceur ou l'infini des sons
> Le doux prolongement mystérieux du rêve.

And rhyme sometimes lends to the sense which it completes, by its splendor, gentleness or infiniteness of sound, the gentle and mysterious expansion of dream.

This view of rhyme may well explain, in part at least, his manner of composition, as shown in his unfinished sonnets. In them we often find either the rhyming words or the tercets or both. The quatrains were obviously left to be completed last. As we have seen, it is precisely in the tercets that we find the most suggestive elements of his sonnets, partly because they contain the famous last verses with their expanded vision. It has been noted that Heredia more frequently uses masculine rhymes in the quatrains than in the tercets.[17] This implies a tendency toward greater use of feminine rhymes in the tercets. Although it is no longer generally accepted that an "e" after the consonant following the tonic vowel in a rhyme changes the pronunciation in any way, Heredia apparently felt that the "e" might play some part in producing that "gentle and mysterious expansion of dream." It is clear that in his opinion a feminine rhyme added a syllable to the verse.[18]

It is certain that the use of rhyme as a starting point forced him to organize his poems to a considerable extent in terms of sound sequences. Although his poetry lacks the subtle and insinuating musical fluidity of some Symbolist poetry, his conception of the nature of poetry is not altogether different from theirs. He is a perfectionist, a solid craftsman in the construction of individual sonnets and of *Les Trophées* as a whole. But, as we have seen, the principles of this structure are in some ways subtle and associative, and do not always spring from the category of logic, such as chronology for instance. He does not belong to the same family of creative spirits as Verlaine, but there are noticeable affinities between him and Baudelaire, Mallarmé above all, and also Valéry, who shared some of his main ideas on rhyme. Heredia would in all likelihood have agreed with the following pronouncement of Valéry:

Il y a bien plus de chances pour qu'une rime procure une idée (littéraire) que pour trouver la rime à partir de l'idée. Là-dessus repose toute la poésie et particulièrement celle des années 60-80.[19]

Chances are much greater that rhyme will engender a (literary) idea than to find the rhyme by beginning with the idea. This is the basis of all poetry and particularly that of the years 1860-1880.

CHAPTER 7

An Artist in Prose

MOST readers who know the name Heredia are apt to regard him as the author of *Les Trophées* only. His reputation as a poet has obscured the fact that he also wrote prose. Indeed, in the eyes of some, his prose is superior to his poetry. Barbey d'Aurevilly, for example, commenting on Heredia's introduction to, and translation of, Bernal Diaz's history of the exploits of the *conquistadores* in the New World, states that Heredia's prose takes flight more easily than his verse because the former has more soul, more life, and more color.[1] In the strictest sense, perhaps only his poetry can be classed as imaginative writing, since his prose consists almost entirely of translations, discourses, official speeches, literary criticism, and letters. But to the extent that artistic considerations figure prominently either in subject matter or style, much of this prose is outstanding and can be regarded as literary art.

I *Bernal Diaz*

Of Heredia's translations (which are of course from Spanish to French), his greatest achievement is his *Véridique Histoire de la conquête de la Nouvelle-Espagne*, par le capitaine Bernal Diaz del Castillo, l'un des conquérants, traduite de l'espagnol, avec une introduction et des notes par José-Maria de Heredia[2] (True History of the Conquest of New-Spain, by Captain Bernal Diaz del Castillo, one of the conquerors, translated from Spanish, with an introduction and notes by José-Maria de Heredia). This was no small undertaking. It required more than ten years to complete the four volumes, which appeared in 1877, 1879, 1881, and 1887. In a letter of May 10, 1887, Hippolyte Taine informed Heredia that he ranked this work with Cellini's *Memoirs* and Luther's *Table Talk*.[3] The translation was based on the Spanish *Historia verdadera de la conquista de la Nueva España*, published in Madrid in 1630. To the more than 1,500 pages of translation, Heredia had added an introduction of over sixty pages and almost a hundred pages of copious and well-documented notes. Altogether the work contains more pages than there are lines in the sonnets of *Les Trophées*.

The long title of this work reveals its subject and the identity of its author. Bernal Diaz dates the book February 26, 1568. At that time he was over seventy years old. His active life as a *conquistador* had ended and he had decided to put aside his sword and take up the pen to compose his account of the conquest of New-Spain so that, according to Heredia, men might remind themselves in times to come as they read the story of his heroic actions that these were the things Bernal Diaz del Castillo had done.[4] The account begins with the year 1514, when an expedition under Captain General Pedro Arias de Avila left Seville for Darien (later known as *la Castille d'Or*). On board was a young man, scarcely twenty-three years of age, unknown, nourished by tales of the fabulous New World, poor, but vigorous and full of a zest for life and what Heredia calls a heroic curiosity. This was Bernal Diaz, companion in arms and friend of such legendary conquerors as Balboa, Alvarado, Sandoval, and Cortes, and who was to become regent of Santiago de Guatemala. His story is that of the discovery and conquest of New-Spain, of the taking of Mexico City, of the restoration of peace, and of Spanish colonization. We follow him in his adventures from his first meeting with the inhabitants of the New World to the many battles in which he engaged. We see the land of the Aztecs with their culture combining elegance and cruelty. With him we contemplate the empire of Anahuac, see Montezuma dead, Mexico in ashes, princes enslaved, chiefs butchered, women captured, and we share his indignation at the torture of the last king of the Aztecs.

This was a chapter in history which intrigued Heredia. It is easy to imagine that he would personally have liked to participate in these adventures. Himself a descendant of the *conquistadores*, as already mentioned, he was not so different from Bernal Diaz in temperament. They shared the same appetite for heroism, the same fiery blood. It is not surprising that he could identify so easily with the subject, treating it almost as his own, as if it were his personal narrative rather than a translation.

Yet it is a translation, and a remarkably good one, not only because Heredia was so strongly attracted to the subject but also because he used all his linguistic skills to preserve the meaning and the flavor of the original. His personality is not completely absent

from the translation in that he tends at times to heighten the color of
the account. The painter constantly lurks behind the narrator, but
we sense that Heredia's tendency toward colorful exuberance is not
allowed to go beyond the bounds of good taste. In spite of the absence of formal limitations in dealing with the
vast scope offered by the subject, Heredia was still forced to dis-
cipline himself in order to maintain the naive simplicity of the
original. To give the illusion of the old Castillian language, he
borrows freely from sixteenth-century French, often omitting articles, and in general lending a slightly archaic flavor to the
language. To give some notion of his language and also of the
simplicity of Bernal Diaz's account, here are the opening sentences
of the narrative:

En l'an mil cinq cent et quatorze, je sortis de Castille en compagnie du
gouvernant Pedro Arias de Avila, à qui pour lors venait d'être donné le
gouvernement de Terre-Ferme. Et venant par la mer, tantôt avec bon vent,
tantôt avec vent contraire, nous arrivâmes à Nombre de Dios. Et en ce temps
il y eut une pestilence dont moururent beaucoup de nos soldats. En outre
nous tombâmes tous malades, et de mauvaises plaies nous venaient aux
jambes. Et, à la même époque, le Gouverneur eut des démêlés avec un
hidalgo qui était Capitaine en cette province, qu'il avait conquise, et se
nommait Vasco Nuñez de Balboa, homme riche, avec qui Pedro Aria de
Avila maria une sienne fille vierge (I, 9).

In the year one thousand five hundred and fourteen, I left Castille in the
company of the governor Pedro Arias de Avila, to whom at that time had just
been given the governorship of Terra-Ferma. And coming by sea, sometimes
with favoring winds, sometimes with contrary ones, we arrived at Nombre
de Dios. And at this time there was a pestilence of which many of our
soldiers died. Besides that we all fell ill and bad sores appeared on our legs.
And at the same time the Governor had squabbles with a hidalgo who was
Captain in that province, which he had conquered, and was named Vasco
Nuñez de Balboa, a rich man, to whom Pedro Arias de Avila married a virgin
daughter of his.

Perhaps Heredia's prose at its best is to be found in his introduction at the beginning of the first volume of the translation. Such men
as Barbey d'Aurevilly and Littré praised it, and Heredia's daughter
Gérard d'Houville calls it "un étonnant chef-d'oeuvre" (an
astonishing masterpiece).[5] But the greatest tribute of all was paid by
Flaubert, that superb prose stylist, who, it is said, used to recite
passages of it by heart in Princess Mathilde's salon.[6]

The main section of the introduction is entitled "Tableau de
l'Espagne de 1513 - 1514," which is followed by a much shorter "La
Jeunesse de Cortes." The purpose of these *tableaux* is to provide the
historical background of the events which Bernal Diaz relates, and to
convey the spirit of the times, particularly the mentality of the *conquistadores* themselves, already so well evoked in the sonnet "Les
Conquérants." Heredia begins with the death of Queen Isabella,
November 26, 1504, and then describes the problems confronting
Ferdinand, left to reign alone. These include his marriage to the
frivolous Germaine de Foix, his disagreements at court, and the un-
rest in the colony of Darien. Ferdinand deals with the latter by
choosing a new captain-general who is to lead an immense Armada
to Darien, restore order, make new discoveries, and act as governor
of the colony. His choice was Pedro Arias de Avila. Heredia then
describes other preparations for the expedition, including the ap-
pointment of a bishop, treasurer, receiver, factor, and supervisor of
the gold foundries, all officers to serve in the colony. Provision is also
made for other needs, and detailed instructions are given to the new
captain-general concerning the expansion of the Church, the conver-
sion of the natives, the morals of the colonists and the founding of a
hospital. The itinerary of the vessels is determined also. The expedition is to set out from Seville, which takes on a new life and excitement with the arrival of Pedro Arias in 1513.

The whole spirit of the Spain of this era is embodied in the life of
Séville prior to the departure of the Armada. "Séville vécut alors
dans une longue fête" (Life in Seville was a long celebration),
observes Heredia (I, xxxvi). But it was not a tranquil time in spite of
the holiday atmosphere. Along with the feverish activity of the
preparations, Heredia evokes all the movement, color and passions
of human life in Seville at the time. He makes us see the tortuous
streets of the ill-famed and dark sections of the city, old women crying out their wares, others "more sorceresses than madonnas" selling
amulets and magic potions, men in capes, smoky lamps and Moorish
courtyards. We hear laughter, cries, hand clapping, castanets and
guitars. Odors of orange blossoms, violent dances, wine, warm gusts
of air, and swirling skirts all add to the variety and multiplicity of
sensuous impressions and help to inflame men already obsessed by
"une convoitise héroïque et brutale" (a heroic and brutal
covetousness) at the prospect of the expedition to the rich New
World. But alas, the dreams of more than one of these *conquistadores* are doomed to end in blood on Spanish soil, for added to

all the other passions are those aroused by the seductive Andalusian women, those snares of Satan who lead the race of Adam to hell's flames and set men's passions on fire to the point where one word or even one gesture may cause swords to be drawn and plunged into warm bodies. Here at last Heredia was free to accumulate details, to paint vast frescoes, to show large crowds in movement, and to permeate everything with what Barbey d'Aurevilly aptly calls Spanish color, which reddens everything "et flambe et fume dans chacune de ses phrases comme du sang de taureau versé . . ." (and flames and smokes in each of his sentences like the blood shed by a bull).[7]

The impression of vibrant life in this scene from the history of Spain owes not a little to Heredia's style. Even objects become more life-like in passages where he makes them the subject of sentences, as for example in this reference to the Alcazar:

Derrière la cathédrale, l'Alcazar, miracle de pierre ouvragée . . . leur ouvrait ses allées pavées de briques . . . (pp. xxiii-xxiv).

Behind the cathedral, the Alcazar, a miracle of wrought stone . . . opened up to them its alleys paved with bricks . . .

He underlines the abundance and richness of the life of the port by means of enumeration:

On y débarquait des vivres, des tonneaux de vin, des barils de farine, de l'artillerie venue de Malaga, des canons de bronze et des fauconneaux, de la poudre, du nitre, du soufre, des houes, des pioches, des bêches, et autres outils . . . (p. xxiv).

There they were unloading food, casks of wine, barrels of flour, artillery from Malaga, bronze cannons and light cannons, powder, saltpeter, sulphur, hoes, pickaxes, spades and other tools . . .

On occasion Heredia heightens the interest of the scene by noting some striking or unusual detail, as for example his observation of the Moorish women pulling their breasts in order to stretch them to try to make them larger and more pendant, a practice which apparently was regarded among the Moors as enhancing their beauty. At times he lends a lightness of touch to expository passages through a kind of Voltairean understatement. For instance, in referring to the Inquisition of the late fifteenth century he first emphasizes its terror and harshness in short staccato sentences and states that for some eighteen years more than 6,000 victims were burned each year either bodily or in effigy, or sentenced to life imprisonment or torture. He then adds the following comment:

Sous l'archevêque Dezza, le feu du zèle sacré s'était fort ralenti. Il n'allumait plus guère que trente-deux bûchers annuels (p. xxi).

Under Archbishop Dezza, the fire of the holy zeal had slowed down greatly. He was no longer lighting any more than a bare thirty-two fires annually.

Heredia is concerned not only with richness of detail but also with its precision. To this end his historical studies and thorough documentation stood him in good stead. In a passage describing the massing of arms for the expedition, for example, he not only lists more than a dozen items, but makes subtle distinctions among those which are closely interrelated and explains the particular use of some of them in the specific circumstances in which they will be employed in the New World.

The historical value of Heredia's introduction may be open to question. A historian's judgments and generalizations are not much in evidence, though they are not entirely absent. After remarking that Cortes was not touched by the magnificence of the tropical land in the New World, Heredia makes the statement that men of action are rarely sensitive to the beauty of things. This seems a broad generalization indeed. But in his appraisal of men, whatever the historical accuracy of these judgments may be, Heredia usually finds a striking formulation for his thought. Thus, in attempting to identify Cortes' outstanding characteristic, he says,

Moins sublime que Colomb, plus heureux et non moins grand que Balboa, Cortes eut la faculté suprême qui manqua toujours à son rival, le grossier Pizarre: il sut grandir avec sa fortune (p. lxiii).

Less sublime than Columbus, more fortunate and not less great than Balboa, Cortes had the supreme faculty which was always lacking in his rival, the coarse Pizarro: he knew how to rise with his fortune.

If it is enough to evoke the atmosphere, the pervading spirit of a moment in time at a given place, then this introduction can qualify as history. But it is above all a picture, and more than that, it is outstanding prose.

II   La Nonne Alferez

Heredia's most important translation aside from Bernal Diaz's history was *La Nonne Alferez*, published by Lemerre in 1894. It appeared first, however, in the *Revue des deux mondes* in March of the same year. The story of the nun Alferez had been in existence for more than two centuries already. Documents included a manuscript of the historian Muñoz and a relation published in Madrid in 1625 under the title *Vida y sucesos de la Monja Alferez doña Catalina de Araujo (Erauso), doncella natural de San Sebastian, escrita por ella misma* (Life and activities of the nun Alferez, Doña Catalina de Araujo (Erauso), damsel born in San Sebastian, written by herself). But Heredia's translation was based on a version which was published in 1829 by Didot in Paris, entitled *Historia de la Monja Alferez, doña Catalina de Erauso, escrita por ella misma.*

In his preface Heredia explains that though it has all the adventure and picaresque characteristics of a cloak and dagger novel, the story of the life of Doña Catalina is true. He underlines her masculinity. More at home with the sword than with the pen, she was homely looking, tall, flat-chested, short-haired, dressed like a man, and looked more like a eunuch or soldier than a woman. In two terse sentences Heredia sums up both her character and that of the story she purportedly wrote:

Ce récit naïf et brutal reflète rapidement son âme et sa vie. Elles furent d'un homme d'action (p. vii).

This naive and brutal narrative gives a rapid reflection of her soul and her life. Both were those of a man of action.

The central fact in her life and the key to her adventures and narrative are to be found precisely in her desire to be a man and in her refusal to play the role of a woman. It is only when she finds herself in peril of death that she speaks of herself as female. She began writing her story in 1624 while returning to Spain by boat. The account of her life begins with her birth and ends with the year 1626 in the month of July, when she was in Naples. An epilogue tells us that at the end she disappears mysteriously, carried off by the devil. Born in San Sebastian de Guipuzcoa in 1585 to Captain Don Miguel de Erauso and Doña Maria Perez de Galarraga y Arce, she is placed in a convent at an early age. At age fifteen she escapes and begins her male life, finding employment first as a page and then as

a cabin boy. From this point her life leads her from one adventure to
another with dazzling rapidity. It is scarcely possible to keep track of
her wanderings. Carthagena, Nombre de Dios, Panama, Paita, Sa⸗
Truxillo, Lima, Paicabi, Tucaman, Potosi, la Plata, Cochabam.
Trinidad, Tenerife, Rome, Naples and Vera Cruz form a list, by no
means exhaustive, of the places she visits. Her experiences include
duels, the threat of a forced marriage to a woman, service in the
army, numerous encounters with officers of the law, prison, and even
the killing of her own brother. Her adventures fall into a pattern,
repeated countless times, of encounters with an enemy, swordplay,
trials, imprisonment and escape. Throughout she thinks of herself as
a man to the point that she seems actually to have convinced herself
that she is one. After a shipwreck in the Lima harbor, for example,
she reports thus:

Seuls, trois hommes purent s'échapper en nageant vers un navire ennemi qui
les recueillit. C'était moi, un Franciscain déchaux et un soldat (p. 112).

Altogether only three men were able to escape by swimming to an enemy
vessel which picked them up. They were myself, a discalced Franciscan and
a soldier.

This tale of extraordinary adventures with its swiftness of movement, its exaggeration, and what at times seems like a caricature of
reality, recalls stories such as Voltaire's *Candide*. But the
philosophical dimension is totally lacking. One would think the story
too incredible to read. Furthermore it has an archaic ring about it,
due to Heredia's use of old words no longer current in French, such
as "partance," "oncques," "occisant" and "choir" for
"départ," "jamais," "tuant" and "tomber," respectively. The
miracle, for which Heredia must take at least some of the credit, is
that somehow the tale does not seem unreal. The narrative is conveyed in language which makes everything appear natural and simple, rather than invented. The numerous chapters into which it is
chopped up underline its general staccato character. Perhaps it is
this fragmentation and also the impression that the action always occurs at a full gallop, which do not allow the reader the opportunity to
stop long enough to become aware of its unreality.

III   Les Bucoliques

When death overtook Heredia in 1905, he was just completing his
edition of André Chénier's *Bucoliques*, but he did not live to see it

published. Always a lover of beautiful objects, he was scrupulous about the physical aspects of books, such as paper, size of print, ink, and binding, and would have been delighted by the luxury edition, illustrated by Fantin-Latour, which appeared after his death.

Heredia dedicates his edition to the memory of his friend Becq de Fouquières "for their love of André Chénier." In his preface, which he entitles "Le Manuscrit des Bucoliques,"[8] he describes how in the Bibliothèque Nationale he happened to come across the manuscript of *Les Bucoliques,* written on pieces of paper mixed with notes and quotations, prose sketches, and fragments, and how he decided then and there to try to restore order in this material. His aim, he states, is not to create an erudite work, but simply to facilitate above all and to make pleasant the reading of these lovely poems. But if his aims were modest, the problems confronting him were not. He compares his task to the reconstitution of a human statue. However, the problem is more difficult, for at least the shape of the human body is known, while the form Chénier had in mind is not known. He explains that his first step was to copy the manuscripts and to take note of errors of which other editors of Chénier had been guilty. His main problem after that was to arrive at some sort of logical classification, and since all classification is artificial, he decided that the best one would be the clearest one. The result is a grouping into ten divisions as follows: I. Poèmes II. Idylles III. Idylles marines IV. Les Dieux et les Héros V. Nymphes et Satyres VI. L'Amour et les Muses VII. Epigrammes VIII. Fragments et Vers épars IX. Esquisses et Projets, and X. Poésies diverses. In the first group he puts poems of lesser importance, including a few which Chénier had called Idylles. Under "Idylles" he groups more than a dozen poems which seem to create a unified impression. The title "Idylles marines" for the third section had been furnished by Chénier himself. He explains the grouping under "Nymphes et Satyres" by comparing the effect to a window pane or a frieze painted on a Greek vase, evoking intertwined dances of nymphs, forest deities and Amor. Under "Fragments et Vers épars" he places all true fragments, isolated, formless and embryonic verses, grouping them according to subject. The section "Esquisses et Projets" includes mostly prose indicating proposed verse to be written, some never completed and others, as for example "L'Aveugle" and "La Liberté" included as finished poems in other sections of *Les Bucoliques.* The last part groups together poems and fragments of a more modern character, which do not fit in with the "concert de la lyre et des flûtes antiques" (p. xv).

In addition to arranging and classifying, Heredia gives titles to some of the poems and even changes a title now and then when it seems more suitable to him to do so. He also attempts to make Chénier's spelling and capitalization more consistent, although he retains Chénier's punctuation, which he considers very personal. In establishing the text he has used Latouche's editions of 1819 and 1833. He explains his choices, when there are some, in the section called "Notes et Variantes." To the question of dating the poems Heredia attaches little importance. Chénier rarely supplied any dates, and in any case he worked on many poems at the same time.

Finally, in the preface Heredia tries to evaluate Chénier's position as a poet. Heredia admired him greatly and he must have felt a certain kinship of spirit with him too. In characterizing his poetry he singles out a number of qualities which we may find in his own work. For example, he praises Chénier for his evocative power, which he calls "la première des vertus poétiques"[9] (the chief poetic virtue). He calls Chénier's vision plastic and says his genius is essentially objective. His observation that no other poet has sung with so much voluptuousness and pride about nature, youth, love, heroes, gods, justice, and liberty leads him to believe that Chénier holds the same place in French poetry as Virgil held in Latin. Most of these, as we have seen, are subjects dear to Heredia as well. In addition he regards Chénier as an incomparable master of the alexandrine. In sum, he sees him as triple-faceted: his *Iambes* make him a man of his own time, the Revolution; his *Elégies* are an expression of his century, the eighteenth; and his *Bucoliques* make him a man of all ages.

In spite of Heredia's modest pretensions, his edition is prepared with his usual care and meticulous rigor and can readily be regarded as scholarly. And yet, in conformity with his stated intentions, it does convey the impression that his concerns were less scholarly than esthetic, and that he wished above all to present Chénier's poems in the most attractive manner possible.

IV *Heredia's* Discours

Another part of Heredia's prose, small but worth reading, is made up of his published addresses, most of which were delivered as part of his official duties and honors as a member of the French Academy. Encouraged by Leconte de Lisle, Sully-Prudhomme and others, Heredia presented himself as a candidate for the chair of Charles de Mazade in the French Academy. Although he was competing against such outstanding writers as Zola and Verlaine, he was nonetheless elected on the first vote on February 29, 1894. The preparation of his official reception address, which he delivered on May 30, 1895, occupied much of his time in the intervening year. It was difficult to find something laudatory to say about his predecessor, as was the custom, because Mazade had been a journalist and writer of no great distinction.

Yet Heredia's address was an immense success. His skilful oratory, his rich and resonant voice, his attractive physical appearance, his confident manner, his eloquence, his elevated prose and his customary elegance won the admiration of the members of the academy. His solution to the problem of eulogizing someone not too deserving of praise was ingenious. Seizing upon the fact that Mazade had written a book on Lamartine, Heredia paid tribute to this enterprise and went on to eulogize Lamartine, with the result that a large part of his address is devoted to the latter, whose name was like a caress to his ears, bringing back cherished memories of childhood, when Lamartine's was the first poetry he could remember hearing.

When we examine Heredia's address we find ourselves admiring its skilful construction and especially the transition, which is almost a *tour de force*, from Mazade to Lamartine. We notice that besides fulfilling his obligation to speak about Mazade he tells us something about his own conception of poetry in his references to Mazade, who was at best a third-rate poet, and to Lamartine, whom he admired both as a man and a poet. After sketching the ancestry, youth and education of Mazade, he comments on the latter's verse by stating that Mazade was not born to be a poet and that his *Odes* lack "l'invention de l'image, le goût des belles formes, le sens de la beauté et de la musique des mots, tout cet art complexe, naïf et savant, qui prête à l'éternelle poésie, suivant la nature et la qualité de l'artiste qu'elle inspire, un son nouveau, une nouvelle vie"[10] (the invention of images, a taste for beautiful forms, a sense of the beauty and music of words, that whole complex art, simple and learned, which lends to lasting poetry, according to the nature and quality of the artist whom it inspires, a new sound, a new life). He goes on to characterize Mazade as a journalist who through his articles is essentially a historian of the revolutionary and post-revolutionary era. In referring to the important events of the Restoration period Heredia singles out the appearance of Lamartine's *Méditations poétiques* in 1820, and exclaims: "Que M. de Mazade soit béni pour avoir écrit un livre sur Lamartine"[11] (Blessed be Mr. Mazade for having written a book on Lamartine).

From this point onward his address is almost entirely devoted to Lamartine. So smooth is the transition that it is not immediately noticeable that Heredia says nothing further about Mazade's book. Heredia agrees with Mazade's condemnation of poetry which is too personal, in that it is like a public confession. Only genius has the right to say everything, comments Heredia, and then only by generalizing and idealizing the poet's intimate feelings. That is what Lamartine has been able to do. His poetry is like song, spiritualizing everything, and is essentially religious. He is the first French poet to have had the "feeling of the infinite." His poetry, in its "divine simplicity," defies analysis and appears to be artless and spontaneous as if it were not the result of conscious effort. Heredia calls *Jocelyn* the only great modern poem which is at once sublime and familiar, and regards *La Chute d'un Ange*, in spite of its unevenness and hasty workmanship, as the only great epic poem of the century.

Heredia's enthusiasm for Lamartine may seem excessive to us today. Childhood memories and associations may have colored his judgment, at least in degree. On the other hand, his characterization of Lamartine's poetry, when taken as a whole and making allowances for a measure of exaggeration, seems to me to be accurate. Although he has left no systematic body of literary criticism, the remarks he makes concerning Lamartine here, like those on Chénier in the preface to *Les Bucoliques*, like those he makes about several other writers also in other official academic addresses, demonstrate his ability to sum up the essential characteristics of a writer succinctly and to find just the right verbal formulation for his judgment. Occasionally it can be striking and memorable, as for example his contrast between Lamartine and Victor Hugo:

Lamartine est l'Aède, le chanteur sacré qu'inspire un Dieu. Victor Hugo est, au sens antique, le Poète, le faiseur de vers par excellence.[12]

Lamartine is the Aede, the sacred singer inspired by a God. Victor Hugo is, in the sense of antiquity, the Poet, the maker of verse *par excellence*.

He then proceeds to characterize Hugo as a visionary, a master of words, a sovereign artist with outstanding power to objectify or materialize the intangible, the invisible and even nothingness itself.

In another address, on September 2, 1894, at the unveiling of Joachim du Bellay's statue, Heredia referred to du Bellay as one of the founders of French poetry, adding that the appearance of his and

Ronsard's first sonnets marks the birth of French poetry, at a time
when the Pléiade was introducing the most prodigious revolution in
French literary history. Du Bellay's special achievement, according
to Heredia, is his combination of power and delicacy in the sonnet.[13]
    The same year Heredia was also called upon to speak at Leconte
de Lisle's funeral. As we have seen, Leconte de Lisle occupied a
special position in his life. In paying tribute to him as a man and as a
poet, Heredia expresses himself with dignified restraint. Once again
we notice his ability to formulate a concise characterization of a
writer's work. As much as he admired Leconte de Lisle's poetry, he
regarded the man as no less worthy of esteem and affection. In his
address he states that Leconte de Lisle for thirty years had been an
educator and incomparable model for the younger poets, a master
both friendly and fraternal, whose soul was tender and proud and
whose mind was profound and charming. He adds that all those who
knew him loved him and venerated him, and that no man has ever
been more deserving of the "supreme honor of tears."[14]
    A few years later, in 1900, Heredia represented the Academy at
the unveiling of Maupassant's monument at Rouen. These circumstances allowed him more freedom to embellish and to digress in
his address than he had had at Leconte de Lisle's funeral. Rouen had
a personal importance for him: his mother's family was from Normandy and she was born in Rouen. It reminded him also of other
great writers from Normandy, such as Malherbe, Corneille and
Flaubert, with whom Maupassant shared "le goût sobre et classique,
la belle ordonnance architecturale"[15] (sober classical taste, beautiful
architectural order). The beauty of Rouen also makes him think of
nearby Croisset where, he recalls, Flaubert used to walk and put
together cadenced sentences to the rhythm of his footsteps. Heredia
must surely have noticed a similarity between his own relationship
with Leconte de Lisle and that which existed between Maupassant
and Flaubert. He gives considerable prominence to Maupassant's
discipleship under Flaubert and the greater part of his address is
devoted to a characterization of Maupassant's writing as a product to
a large extent of Flaubert's example.
    In a general way Maupassant possessed what Heredia considers to
be the two chief qualities of a creative artist: evocative power and
detachment. Only Flaubert surpassed him in these two areas. But in
his later works Maupassant appears less detached, and for that
reason perhaps, adds Heredia, less moving. In a more specific way,
Maupassant's contribution was his study of "la fille et le paysan"

(the spinster and the peasant). This comment leads Heredia to
observe that while eighteenth-century writers often elevate and
idealize primitive peoples and the Romantics do the same for con-
victs, criminals and prostitutes, some writers in the last half of the
nineteenth century are beginning instead to go down to the level of
"inferior humanity" in order to study it. Heredia's treatment of
Maupassant's personal life, his illness, disordered mind and death is
an example of tact, delicacy and good taste. His comment on
Maupassant's love of nature and fear of death is striking:

Personne n'a plus amèrement compris que ce sensitif exaspéré le fini de la
sensation dans l'infini de la nature dont l'éternel recommencement est la
pire des ironies pour l'homme éphémère.

No one has understood more bitterly than this exasperated and sensitive
man the finite character of sensation within the infinity of nature, whose
eternal renewal is the worst of ironies for ephemeral man.

Is it not precisely that finite man within infinite nature whom we en-
counter at every step in Heredia's *Trophées?*

It is interesting to note that the writers about whom Heredia chose
to write or speak were almost all in some way kindred spirits, and the
qualities he admires in them are often those he cultivated in his own
work, or which we can find there. Thus he has in common with du
Bellay the choice and mastery of the sonnet form, with Lamartine a
certain elevation and dignity, with Chénier and Maupassant objectivity and evocative power, with Chénier in particular mastery of the
alexandrine and a love of antiquity, and with Leconte de Lisle
almost a whole poetic creed.

Heredia's prose as a whole is graceful in style and pleasant to read.
It is provocative too in that it suggests that he might have been an
outstanding prose writer had he chosen to follow such a course. But
although in his various prose writings he indicates directions, he
never quite completes any journey. His story of Bernal Diaz is not
quite history and his translation of the nun Alferez' narrative does
not really show whether he could have written good prose fiction,
although it leads us to suspect that he could have, and in fact the
reader may find himself forgetting that it is a translation. Similarly
his writings on various literary figures do not quite make him a
literary critic, although his scattered observations come close to con-
vincing us that he might have been an excellent one had he committed himself to that path.

CHAPTER 8

Conclusion

I T is fairly generally conceded today that Heredia was Leconte de Lisle's only true disciple and the poet who best put into practice the Parnassian ideal of poetry. Neither of them had any profound influence on the subsequent development of French poetry, in the manner that Hugo or Baudelaire left their mark on it. Heredia founded no school and had no disciples. At most we can find in the poetry of some minor writers of the late nineteenth and early twentieth centuries some elements that recall Heredia. While he was alive his influence made itself felt through his personality, in his encouragement of younger poets, and through his own enthusiasm and willingness to consider new approaches, an attitude which won him the respect of the Symbolists and put him into a position resembling that of a transition figure. Indeed, Henri de Régnier regarded *Les Trophées* as the link between two kinds of poetry, Parnassian and Symbolist, much as Chénier's *Bucoliques* had led from Classical to Romantic poetry.[1] However, even when all this is said, few would maintain seriously that Heredia in any significant way affected the direction of the main stream of poetry in France.

We have seen that when *Les Trophées* appeared in 1893, the collection was an instant and unqualified success. But now, more than a half century later, Heredia is little read and little studied, even by literary scholars. Perhaps as a poet he deserves a better fate, but in art as in life destiny cannot be legislated. He is neither a great prose writer nor a great poet, although he is a first-rate prose stylist and an artist of the first order in poetry. In his prose he is neither a novelist, nor a short story writer, nor a historian, nor a critic, nor an essayist, yet his prose contains elements of all of these. We sense that he might have risen to greater heights had he seriously committed himself to any one of these genres. His poetic virtuosity is unquestionable. Color, perfection of form and suggestive effects are all flawlessly present in his sonnets.

Paradoxically this very perfection proves to be after all a weakness in his poetry. Too much sustained perfection can result in a kind of uniformity comparable to that which we might find in a piece of music without rests and without dynamics. More half tones, some relaxation of the sustained level, might well have added to, rather than detracted from, the esthetic impact of his poetry. It has been noted, for example, that the word "petit," which might have provided some relief from uniformly vast dimensions, does not appear even once in Les Trophées.[2] Even though much of his poetry has suggestive power, we may sometimes feel that even that effect is somewhat too calculated. His conception of poetry is at the opposite pole to that which Verlaine expresses near the end of his well known "Art poétique":

> Que ton vers soit la bonne aventure
> Éparse au vent crispé du matin
> Qui va fleurant la menthe et le thym —

Let your verse be the lucky chance scattered to the brisk morning wind which passes fragrant with mint and thyme.

It was the same Verlaine, a Symbolist, who praised Heredia's verse for its perfection, its nobility, its vigor, its purity, its richness of sonorities and sensations, its freedom from vulgarity of any sort, its tenderness underlying its elevation, but above all, its heroism. This judgment is echoed by Gérard d'Houville, who states that Les Trophées are for heroes and that during World War I soldiers found inspiration in them, in the vision of the somber greatness of history with its inflexible bonds linking past to future, and in the virtues of stoic endurance, of the acceptance of themselves and of serene renunciation.[3] These judgments constitute high praise, but seen through twentieth-century eyes they may be less laudatory. An age whose poetry still owes something to Baudelaire's Fleurs du mal may have reservations about the uniform purity of Heredia's verse and may judge it to be a weakness that his poetry contains no sense for the satanic, little awareness of the temptations of the flesh and no attempt to explore the esthetic possibilities of evil.

It is possible also that the twentieth century is less impressed by heroism and nobility. Many would contend that it is not a heroic age, much less an aristocratic one, and that those ideals belong to the past. However that may be, it seems to me that when we read Les Trophées we are left with a curious sense of distance. To us, accustomed as we are to modern literature of commitment and concern for contemporary social problems, Heredia may seem strangely detached. Not only does he show no interest in social reform, but his attitude toward any imperfections in life is never one of indignation. The sense of distance comes most obviously from the historical perspective of *Les Trophées*, which of course stop with the Renaissance, if we exclude "La Nature et le Rêve," whose historical situation is indefinite. But perhaps even more important is that lack of immediacy which may derive from excessive distillation of personal emotion. Heredia's love of life and beauty, together with his awareness that life and beauty must pass, are embodied in many unforgettable verses. When we lay down the book we can still hear the limitless ocean weeping for the Sirens, and see the city of Carthagena sleeping under Caribbean palm trees. But perhaps readers could wish that Heredia somehow had managed to inject now and then some ingredient which would have made the vision a little less serene.

It may be argued that his very conception of poetry is not modern. But I do not think the case is clear cut. In some important ways his conception was not so different from that of Mallarmé or Valéry, although his recorded reflections on the nature of poetry are slight in comparison with theirs. Still he shared with them the concept of "the difficult art" as opposed to undisciplined spontaneity. I think he would have agreed with Mallarmé's comment that sonnets are made with words, not with ideas. His unfinished sonnets show that his point of departure was key rhyme words and suggestive images rather than ideas. On the question of rhyme he was very close to Valéry, as we have seen. Clearly words as objects in themselves were important to him, like a beautiful vase, an inlaid dagger, a Renaissance painting or a richly bound book.

Jules Lemaître closes a study of Heredia with these words:

Je ne lui demande qu'une chose: Qu'il continue de feuilleter le soir avant de s'endormir, des catalogues d'épées, d'armures et de meubles anciens, rien de mieux; mais qu'il s'accoude plus souvent sur la roche moussue où rêve Sabinula.[4]

I ask only one thing of him: Let him continue to look through catalogues of swords, arms and old furniture in the evening before going to sleep, fine; but let him more often lean on the mossy rock where Sabinula dreams.

The reference is to the sonnet "L'Exilée," evoking a woman's nightly nostalgia for the Rome from which she was exiled.

Lemaître's remark is to the point. It identifies two kinds of poetic worlds. One is that of beautiful objects, produced by exquisite craftsmanship, existing in a sculptural order of forms and colors, but in a sense distant because it is a world outside of us. The other is the world of dream, the inner world, more intangible, more nebulous, having that subtle quality of which music is perhaps the most perfect artistic expression. What Lemaître seems to be saying is that in *Les Trophées* the first of these poetic worlds dominates and that he wishes that Heredia might have concentrated more on the second.

Many readers are likely to share Lemaître's view, at least as a first impression. There is no doubt that in *Les Trophées* objects, images, tableaux, forms and colors are prominent. But the inner world, without which the other would have little meaning, is there too, less noticeable perhaps and discreetly unobtrusive because it is underlying. And being underlying it is basic, and in a sense splendidly human. When we learn to move in Heredia's world we realize that each statue, each landscape, each battle, each objective manifestation of life relates to the most human of issues, the beauty of life and the regret that it does not endure. The world of human dreams and emotions can be discovered through the objects which guide us to them. An ocean lamenting the days of Sirens suffices to produce a vision of immense space and time and the melancholy of its passing. A sleeping city, like an island in time, is another expression of the serene sadness of dying. A late autumn petal of a faded flower awakens tender nostalgia for a distant childhood home. A child weeping over the grave of a grasshopper conveys in an exquisitely touching manner the reality of death. These are only a few examples. In spite of this surprising variety of registers of human emotions, Heredia bypasses contemporary issues, as being of brief and superficial importance.

The emotional effect of *Les Trophées* is not one of existential anguish, of social indignation, nor of despair. But there is an undertone of melancholy nonetheless, not very obvious perhaps, but present everywhere. It is the melancholy of a human being who loves life and beauty intensely, but who, contemplating them from a kind of timeless perspective, has learned to accept without anger and bitterness the fact that nothing human will last. It is doubtful whether Heredia will ever be widely read. But for those who appreciate the highest quality of workmanship in verbal art, for those who share his aristocratic tastes, and above all for those who love beautiful things and are willing to contemplate human destiny stripped of the accidental trappings of limited time and place, and finally, for those who appreciate the highest art of the sonnet form, Heredia offers rich rewards.

Notes and References

Chapter One

1. I am indebted to the detailed study of Miodrag Ibrovac, *José-Maria de Heredia. Sa Vie, son oeuvre* (Paris: Les Presses françaises, 1923), for much information concerning Heredia's origins and life. Unless otherwise stated, all references to Ibrovac will be to this work.

2. See François de Vaux de Foletier, "Les Ancêtres normands de Heredia," *Revue des deux mondes* (January 1, 1964), pp. 96-108.

3. Henri de Régnier, *Nos Rencontres* (Paris: Mercure de France, 1931), p. 33.

4. For some anecdotes concerning Heredia's childhood see Gérard d'Houville, "A Propos des *Trophées*," *Revue des deux mondes*, XXX (November 15, 1925): 427-435.

5. Quoted by Armand Godoy, "José-Maria de Heredia," *Revue des deux mondes* (November 1, 1955), p. 81.

6. This occurred on at least three occasions (1852, 1853, 1856).

7. Madame Heredia in her letters to Fauvelle repeatedly observes the resemblance between her son and her husband. In a letter of June 22, 1859, cited by Ibrovac, p. 31, she notes that her son takes after his father in that his conversations smack of reason and the desire to have an honorable career.

8. For an informative article on this stage of Heredia's education see Jacques Guignard, "José-Maria de Heredia et l'Ecole des Chartes," *Bibliothèque de l'Ecole des Chartes*, 1944, pp. 215-225.

9. Discours de réception à l'Academie Française," in *Les Trophées* (Paris: Lemerre, n.d. [1944]), p. 231.

10. Heredia in his "Discours," p. 230, mentions the number of pages in this edition of Lamartine.

11. Cited by Ibrovac, p. 38.

12. According to Pierre Louÿs, cited by Godoy, *op. cit.*, p. 81.

13. Ibrovac, pp. 40-42, gives specific verses from Leconte de Lisle, suggested by "Les Bois américains."

14. This poem is quoted by Ibrovac, pp. 40-42.

15. Ibrovac, pp. 61-64.

16. *Ibid.*, p. 56.

Chapter Two

1. Luc Badesco, *La Génération poétique de 1860* (Paris: Nizet, 1971), I: 143.

2. Jules Huret, *Enquête sur l'évolution littéraire* (Paris: Charpentier et Fasquelle, 1894), p. 310.

3. The invention of the name is sometimes attributed to Barbey d'Aurevilly, who in a series of articles in *La Nain jaune* in 1866 (October 27, November 7 and 14) attacked these poets.

4. See Maurice Souriau, *Histoire du Parnasse* (Paris: Spes, 1929), pp. xviii-xxiv.

5. Catulle Mendès, *La Légende du Parnasse contemporain* (Bruxelles: Auguste Brancart, 1884), p. 57.

6. Théophile Gautier, *Histoire du romantisme*, 3rd ed. (Paris: Charpentier, 1887), p. 336.

7. Huret, *op. cit.*, p. 283.

Chapter Three

1. Quoted by Ibrovac, p. 84.

2. Anatole France, *La Vie littéraire*, 3ᵉ série, in *Oeuvres complètes illustrées* (Paris: Calman-Lévy, 1925), VII: 297-298.

3. Cited by Ibrovac, pp. 166-167.

4. Henri de Régnier, *Portraits et souvenirs* (Paris: Mercure de France, 1913), p. 78.

5. Jules Lemaître, *Les Contemporains* (Paris: Société Française d'Imprimerie et de Librairie, 1896), II: 50.

6. Cited by Ibrovac, p. 79.

7. Cited by Badesco, *op. cit.*, II: 1114.

8. Cited by Ibrovac, p. 126.

9. Souriau, *op. cit.*, p. xlii.

10. Cited by Souriau, *op. cit.*, p. 170.

11. All three eventually married literary men of some repute. Hélène became Madame René Doumic; Marie, who was herself a poetess with the pseudonym of Gérard d'Houville, was the wife of Henri de Régnier; and Louise later married Pierre Louÿs.

12. Huret, *op. cit.*, pp. 310-311.

13. See Ibrovac, pp. 287-288, for an outstanding example. He cites a long letter in which Leconte de Lisle criticizes Heredia's "Serrement des mains" and offers corrections in versification, rhythm, harmony and diction.

14. Ibrovac, p. 150.

15. Pierre Flottes, *Leconte de Lisle, l'homme et l'oeuvre* (Paris: Hatier-Boivin, 1954), p. 127.

16. Ibrovac, pp. 175-176.

17. Huret, *op. cit.*, p. 309.

18. Cited by Ibrovac, p. 405.

19. Cited by Ibrovac, p. 198.

20. Ibrovac, p. 197.
21. Cited by Souriau, *op. cit.*, p. 442.

Chapter Four

1. Godoy, *op. cit.*, p. 84.
2. Ibrovac, p. 302.
3. *Ibid.*, p. 303.
4. Ernest Prévost, "José-Maria de Heredia, la vie et l'oeuvre du poète," *Le Figaro* (October 17, 1925).
5. Pierre Louÿs, "Entretiens avec J.-M. de Heredia," *Le Manuscrit autographe*, no. 7 (January-February, 1927): 1.
6. "Mer montante," it may be mentioned in passing, contains some unmistakable echoes of Victor Hugo, recalling among other poems "Paroles sur la dune" and "Ce qu'on entend sur la montagne."
7. Miodrag Ibrovac, *José-Maria de Heredia. Les Sources des "Trophées"* (Paris: Les Presses françaises, 1923), p. 164.
8. For examples see Ibrovac, pp. 164-169, passim.
9. Lemaître, *op. cit.*, p. 63.

Chapter Five

1. For a detailed treatment of the nineteenth-century French epic see Herbert Hunt, *The Epic in Nineteenth-Century France* (Blackwell: Oxford, 1941).
2. Cited by Ibrovac, p. 388.
3. Quoted by Thomas Seccombe and Louis Brandin, "José-Maria de Heredia 1842-1905. The Evolution of the Sonnet," *The Fortnightly Review*, LXXVIII (December, 1905): 1081.
4. "Discours de réception . . . ," p. 219.
5. It should be noted that Heredia was not a French national and was not naturalized until after the publication of *Les Trophées*.
6. Gérard d'Houville, *op. cit.*, p. 429.
7. J. C. Bailey, "The Sonnets of M. de Heredia," *The Fortnightly Review*, XXIV (July - December, 1898): 384.
8. Cited by Gaston Picard, "Eloge de José-Maria de Heredia par Verlaine," *Le Figaro* (October 17, 1925).
9. René Doumic, "José-Maria de Heredia," *Revue des deux mondes*, XXIX (October 15, 1905): 931.
10. Cited by Ibrovac, p. 386.

Chapter Six

1. Hunt, *op. cit.*, pp. 353-354.
2. A well-known history of the sonnet is Max Jasinski's, *Histoire du sonnet en France* (Douai, 1903; reprint ed., Geneva: Slatkine, 1970).
3. Henri Morier, *Dictionnaire de poétique et de rhétorique* (Paris: Presses Universitaires de France, 1961), p. 396.

4. René Doumic, "Une Histoire du sonnet," *Revue des deux mondes*, XX (March 15, 1904): 455.

5. Cited by Ibrovac, p. 331.

6. U.-V. Chatelain, *José-Maria de Heredia. Sa Vie et son milieu* (Paris: Cahiers des études littéraires françaises, 1930), footnote p. 15.

7. Gérard d'Houville, *op. cit.*, p. 430.

8. Seccombe and Brandin, *op. cit.*, p. 1074.

9. Edmund Gosse, "The New Immortal J.-M. de Heredia," *The Contemporary Review*, LXV (April, 1894): 475.

10. Cited by Ibrovac, p. 488.

11. A. R. Chisholm, "Towards an Analytical Criticism of Poetry," *Australian Universities Modern Language Association*, no. 22 (1964): 170.

12. A. R. Chisholm, "A Secret of Heredia's Art," *Modern Language Review*, XXVI (1931): 159.

13. Jules Lemaître, *op. cit.*, II: 56.

14. Jean Royère, *Le Point de vue de Sirius* (Paris: Messein, 1935), p. 42.

15. Huret, *op. cit.*, p. 304.

16. Cited by Ibrovac, p. 471.

17. Ibrovac, pp. 474-475.

18. See the Preface to André Chénier, *Les Bucoliques*, ed. José-Maria de Heredia (Paris: Maison du Livre, 1907), p. xxix.

19. Valéry, "Cahiers B 1910," *Tel Quel I* (Paris: Nouvelle Revue Française, 1941), p. 203.

Chapter Seven

1. Jules-Amédée Barbey d'Aurevilly, *Poésie et Poètes* (Paris: Lemerre, 1906), p. 314.

2. 4 vols., Paris: Lemerre, 1877 - 1887.

3. *Taine, Sa Vie et sa correspondance* (Paris: Hachette, 1907), IV: 237.

4. *Véridique Histoire*, I: xlix.

5. Gérard d'Houville, *op. cit.*, p. 429.

6. Ibrovac, p. 156.

7. Barbey d'Aurevilly, *op. cit.*, p. 320.

8. In André Chénier, *Les Bucoliques*, publiées d'après le manuscrit original dans un ordre nouveau avec une préface et des notes par José-Maria de Heredia de l'Académie Française (Paris: Maison du Livre, 1907).

9. *Ibid.*, xxvi.

10. "Discours de réception . . . ," p. 220.

11. *Ibid.*, p. 231.

12. *Ibid.*, p. 232.

13. *Institut de France. Discours prononcé à l'inauguration de la statue de Joachim du Bellay à Ancenis* (Paris: Firmin-Didot, 1894), p. 5.

14. *Institut de France. Académie Française. Funérailles de M. Leconte de Lisle. Discours de M. de Heredia* (Paris: Firmin-Didot, 1894).

15. "Guy de Maupassant," *Le Journal* (May 28, 1900), p. 1. The whole address is found on this page.

Chapter Eight

1. Cited by Pierre Martino, *Parnasse et Symbolisme* (Paris: Armand Colin, 1958), p. 85.

2. Heinrich Fromm, *"Les Trophées" von José-Maria de Heredia. Untersuchungen über den Aufbau, Reim und Stil* (Greifswald: University of Greifswald dissertation, 1913), cited by Ibrovac, p. 426.

3. Gérard d'Houville, *op. cit.*, p. 434.

4. Jules Lemaître, *op. cit.*, p. 65.

Bibliography

PRIMARY SOURCES

Place of publication is Paris unless otherwise stated.

1. Poetry
   The following list does not contain non-commercial editions brought out in small numbers, nor does it include all the reprintings of undated Lemerre editions.
Les Trophées, Lemerre, 1893.
Oeuvres de José-Maria de Heredia. Les Trophées. Lemerre, 1895.
Les Trophées. Lemerre, n.d. [1920]. This edition contains "Salut à l'empereur" and "Discours de réception à l'Académie Française."
Poésies complètes de José-Maria de Heredia. Les Trophées. Lemerre, 1924. A number of previously unpublished poems have been added in this edition.
Les Trophées, ed. F. W. Stockoe. Cambridge: Cambridge University Press, 1942.
Les Trophées. Lemerre, n.d. [1944]. Contains "Discours de réception à l'Académie Française."
Les Trophées, Collection Poche-Club, 38. Nouvel Office d'Edition, 1965.
Les Trophées, Collection Club des Chefs-d'Oeuvre. Pierre Belfond, 1965.
   A list of isolated published poems not found in *Les Trophées* is contained in the bibliography of Miodrag Ibrovac, *José-Maria de Heredia. Sa Vie, son oeuvre.* Les Presses françaises, 1923.
   Translations into English:
Sonnets from the "Trophies" of José-Maria de Heredia, rendered into English by Edward Robeson Taylor. San Francisco: Paul Elder, 1902.
Translations from José-Maria de Heredia, by Merle St. Croix Wright. New York: H. Vinal Ltd., 1927.
Les Trophées, Fifty Sonnets by José-Maria de Heredia, translated and introduced by Brian Hill. London: Rupert Hart-Davis, 1962.
Les Trophées, José-Maria de Heredia, the Sonnets, translated by Henry Johnson. Brunswick, Me.: F. C. Chandler and Son, 1910.

Les Trophées, Sonnets by José-Maria de Heredia, translated by Frank Sewall. Boston: Small, Maynard and Company, 1900.

The Trophies, with other Sonnets by José-Maria de Heredia, now first completely translated into English by John Myers O'Hara and John Hervey. New York: The John Day Company, 1929.

2. Prose

The most comprehensive list of Heredia's prose writings, including a few letters, prefaces, addresses and translations, can be found in Ibrovac, pp. 594-600. His correspondence, which is scanty by most standards, has not been collected for publication. I offer below those items which I regard as his most important prose writings according to scope, artistic merit, and ideas concerning literature and art.

Chénier, André. *Les Bucoliques,* publiées d'après le manuscrit original dans un ordre nouveau avec une préface et des notes par José-Maria de Heredia de l'Académie Française. Maison du Livre, 1907. The first edition appeared in 1905 with a dedication to Becq de Fouquières. The preface was also published separately under the title "Le Manuscrit des *Bucoliques*," in the *Revue des deux mondes,* XXX (November 1, 1905): 146-167.

"Discours de réception à l'Académie Française," in *Institut de France. Académie Française. Discours prononcés dans la séance publique tenue par l'Académie Française pour la réception de M. José-Maria de Heredia, le jeudi 30 mai 1895.* Firmin-Didot, 1895. This may also be found in several editions of *Les Trophées.*

Institut de France. Académie Française. Inauguration de la statue de Joachim du Bellay à Ancenis, le dimanche 2 septembre 1894. Discours de M. de Heredia. Firmin-Didot, 1894.

Institut de France. Académie Française. Funérailles de M. Leconte de Lisle. Discours de M. de Heredia. Firmin-Didot, 1894.

"Guy de Maupassant," *Le Journal,* May 28, 1900, p. 1.

Translations from Spanish to French:

La Nonne Alferez, par Catalina de Erauso, illustrations de Daniel Vierge gravées par Privat-Richard. Lemerre, 1894. This also appeared in the *Revue des deux mondes,* March 1, 1894, pp. 121-161.

Véridique Histoire de la conquête de la Nouvelle-Espagne, par le capitaine Bernal Diaz de Castillo, l'un des conquérants, traduite de l'espagnol avec une introduction et des notes par José-Maria de Heredia. 4 vols. Lemerre, 1877-1887.

SECONDARY SOURCES

1. On Heredia

BAILEY, J. C. "The Sonnets of M. de Heredia," *The Fortnightly Review,* September 1898, pp. 369-384. An appreciation of Heredia's affinities with the spirit of the Renaissance.

CHATELAIN, U.-V. *José-Maria de Heredia. Sa Vie et son milieu.* Paris:

Cahiers des études littéraires françaises, 1930. A rather brief study. Some interesting observations on Heredia's versatility as a poet.

CHISHOLM, A. R. "A Secret of Heredia's Art," *Modern Language Review*, XXVI (1931): 159-169.

——. "Towards an Analytical Criticism of Poetry," *Australian Universities Modern Language Association*, no. 22 (November, 1964): 164-177. These two articles study mirror images in Heredia's sonnets.

FROMM, HEINRICH. *"Les Trophées" von José-Maria de Heredia. Untersuchungen über den Aufbau, Reim und Stil.* Greifswald: University of Greifswald dissertation, 1913. In some ways a superficial study, but detailed in questions of rhyme and versification, although it tends to be a bit mechanical.

GOSSE, EDMUND. "The New Immortal. J.-M. de Heredia," *The Contemporary Review*, LXV (April, 1894): 471-482. Identifies Heredia's particular strengths and weaknesses.

GUIGNARD, JACQUES. "José-Maria de Heredia et l'Ecole des Chartes," *Bibliothèque de l'Ecole des Chartes*, 1944, pp. 215-225. Contains little known facts on this part of Heredia's life. Jacques Guignard is the present chief administrator of the Bibliothèque de l'Arsenal, a position Heredia held at the time of his death.

IBROVAC, MIODRAG. *José-Maria de Heredia. Les Sources des "Trophées."* Paris: Les Presses françaises, 1923. An exhaustive study indicating probable sources for the sonnets in *Les Trophées*.

——. *José-Maria de Heredia. Sa Vie, son oeuvre.* Paris: Les Presses françaises, 1923. The most complete study of Heredia's life and work so far. It is generally excellent, contains a wealth of information, solid documentation, and a very good bibliography.

MOUSSAT, E. *Les Sonnets de José-Maria de Heredia.* Paris: Foucher, n.d. [1949]. An elementary approach in the school series "Expliquez-moi. . . ."

SECCOMBE, THOMAS and LOUIS BRANDIN. "José-Maria de Heredia, 1842-1905. The Evolution of the Sonnet," *The Fortnightly Review*, LXXVIII (December, 1905): 1074-1087. Remarkably informative, concise and well-balanced study.

SUCHAJ, MARGARET MARY. *L'Esthétique du Parnasse étudiée à travers "Les Trophées" de José-Maria de Heredia,* unpublished master's thesis, University of Manitoba, 1965. A well done piece of work on a small scale, but does not cover much new ground.

TALMEYR, MAURICE. "J.-M. de Heredia prosateur. *La Nonne Alferez,*" *Le Figaro*, November 7, 1925. Speculates that *La Nonne Alferez* may not be a translation, but an original creation of Heredia.

2. More general studies

BARBEY d'AUREVILLY, JULES-AMEDEE. *Poésie et poètes.* Paris: Lemerre, 1906. Perhaps biased because of Barbey d'Aurevilly's general hostility toward Parnassian poetry.

CHARLTON, DONALD G. *Positivist Thought in France during the Second Empire 1852-1870.* Oxford: Clarendon Press, 1959. Although this book contains only brief references to Heredia, it provides much valuable insight into the intellectual climate of his age.

DENOMME, ROBERT T. *The French Parnassian Poets.* Carbondale and Edwardsville: Southern Illinois University Press, and London and Amsterdam: Feffer and Simons, Inc., 1972. A recent book which situates Parnassian poetry in the positivist and realist current. Good studies of some individual Parnassian poets. Analyses of a few of Heredia's sonnets.

HUNT, HERBERT. *The Epic in Nineteenth-Century France.* Oxford: Blackwell, 1941. Still one of the best studies on the subject.

HURET, JULES. *Enquête sur l'évolution littéraire.* Paris: Charpentier et Fasquelle, 1894. Contains reports of interviews with writers of Heredia's time, including Heredia himself.

JASINSKI, MAX. *Histoire du sonnet en France.* Geneva: Slatkine Reprints, 1970. A well-known history of the sonnet in France, dedicated to Heredia.

ROYERE, JEAN. *Le Point de vue de Sirius.* Paris: Messein, 1935. Contains a stimulating study attempting to demonstrate links between Heredia and Mallarmé.

SCHAFFER, AARON. "The Parnassians at Play," *Romanic Review,* XXI (1930): 49-59. Contains information on Parnassian social and literary activities, including the preparation of journals.

SOURIAU, MAURICE. *Histoire du Parnasse.* Paris: Spes, 1929. Probably the best known and most complete history of the Parnassians in France.

VINCENT, FRANCIS. *Les Parnassiens. L'Esthétique de l'école. Les Oeuvres et les hommes.* Paris: Gabriel Beauchesne et ses fils, 1933. A more succinct study of the Parnassians than Souriau's book.

Index

(The works of Heredia are listed under his name)